First Published in 2016

ISBN 978-00728815-7-9

Printed in the United States of America

First Printing June 2016

Cover Photo Myrtle Beach: Joe Zunker

Proof Readers: Nancy Sanderson

Alice Dorsher

I love **story**.

I learn better, faster and easier through **story.**

Each **story** is personally our very own... just as each life is an individual experience perceived through our own filters ... so are our **stories**.

So, in this book are some of my **stories**.

I try to keep each experience as factual as possible... through the days, weeks and years of ordinary life, I go to my computer and quickly create a file with only facts about an event. If one of my sons is telling me a **story**, I will take a scrap of paper, write a few notes and later create a file. I do this so routinely that those files have been forgotten for years ... nearly fifteen years actually ... my file is one of those things that I kept telling myself, "I'll just keep collecting these tidbits and someday I'll write another book".

Then one fateful day, months ago, I opened that file to find treasures beyond belief. It is from this large file that this book was written ... an electronic file much like a box at the back of the closet ... the place you store your favorite old baby blanket or your worn out teddy bear from childhood ... only mine is a box of recollections.

So these **stories** are dedicated to the main characters in my **stories**.   To my husband Joe.

To my sons John, Rob and Tom.

To my daughter-by-choice, Shannon.

To my grandchildren Brady and Maggie.

The Beach I Walk On

Small Monumental Moments

By Cathy Weber-Zunker

Index

Old Friends 8

Boston Legal 13

In Defense of Weakness 16

Country Girl..20

If That Old Barn Could Talk....................... 23

A Defining Moment....................................26

Standing Alone...29

The T-Shirt...32

Three Sons, One Room...............................35

Misha's Arms...38

John's 13th Christmas.................................41

The Shrek Principle....................................44

The Nudge..47

Playing Hooky..49

Pearl...52

Maggie's Handwriting................................54

Insurance..57

The Fabric Store...59

The Golden Birthday...................................61

Could I Have This Dance?..........................64

A Dream...67

Movie Night...70

A Fairy Tale Moment.. 73

A Hero in a Truck..78

Zephyr Ride..80

Grizzly Adams at Wal Mart... 83

Happy Anniversary..86

Just Buying Eggs...89

Goals..92

Whoa!.. 94

What's For Supper Honey?... 96

Uncle Jim's Wisdom...99

Small Town America..101

The Monument..102

Three Little Angels Hangin' On A Tree 105

The Swill Cart..108

When Maggie Was Seven...111

Smart Maggie..114

Happy Endings...116

A Day with Brady..119

Cinderella (8-2009)...122

Mavericks...125

Choking a Bird..129

By-Invitation-Only..130

Nick..134

Caramel Corn 139

Fathers-of-Daughters 141

Brady's Life Lesson..144

The Baton Man..147

Coincidence..149

At the Library...152

Twindom...154

To My Twin Sister... 155

A Toast to Sisters..156

Target Field..159

Rochester Minnesota..163

Priceless...167

The Power Washer..169

Fire Breathing Dragon..172

John's 16th Birthday 175

Murray..176

Selling Land...179

Will 12 Students Return?...182

Scraps of Paper...187

"He Started It!"..190

2003 193

Ageless Thinking 196

Without Words..200

Ted from Iowa..203

Interstate 35 at 65 MPH.. 205

School Thanksgiving Lunch.................................208

C'mon Big Dog...211

The Grounded Documentary..............................214

Crying Together..217

Our Greatest Fear..219

Unbidden...221

The Best Man's Shirt...224

Brian and Kelley's Wedding...............................229

A Head on His Shoulder....................................232

Chicken Pox..234

Bank Account...237

Maggie April 2016 240

Rock Star 243

For the Love of Gloria....................................... 249

The Dance Card 261

Old Friends

It was an easy task to fly to Arizona, stay for a few days, and then fly home with my grandson in tow. All the Minnesota relatives were anxious to totally spoil him for 3 ½ weeks.

11-year-old Brady had been anticipating this for months.

At the airport, after passing through security, it was just him and me alone. With no competition for air time the young man began to talk – and talk. Before we even found our gate, he asked a question he had asked me at least *three times before*.

8

He asked, "Grandma Cathy, do you know where Chase is?"

In the past, every time he had asked, I just let the question slip away thinking that he would forget about it. I mean really, can his memory really go back to toddler days? Is it possible for an 11 year old to have an *old* friend? They were only 3 ½ years old the last time they saw each other. That means it's been 7 ½ years since Brady played with Chase at daycare. And yet each time Brady comes to MN he asks me the same question.

As kids the two were inseparable. They played with toy telephones and the walkie talkies were their favorite. They liked Legos too, and they had unlimited time to just play. Mostly I remember how inseparable they were at my daycare...Mutt & Jeff, Pete and Repeat. They were loyal to each other too. When I got to take grandson Brady shopping for a toy on the weekend, he would carefully choose something and then say "Buy one for Chasey too!" And so the toy boxes were heavy with duplicate toys, one for Brady and one for Chase.

"Should I try to find him?" I asked.

"Yes" he said simply.

I filed it away in the back of my brain once again.

Nearly a week had passed before the thought resurfaced and I assumed I would make a few attempts and then later would woefully apologize for not being able to find Chase. I doubted that I could find him because I knew that Chase's family had been moving and changing locations several times.

Finally a two day phone trail led me to the director of the agency where Chase's mother works. I explained to the woman on the phone that I was Brady's grandma and that I had had both Brady and Chase in my daycare years ago and now I was trying to find Chase's mother in order to bring the two of them back together. I knew, of course, the director could not give me a phone number nor could she even confirm that Chase's mom worked for the agency...I entrusted her with MY phone numbers hoping my urgency would motivate the director to pass the message along.

At the end of the day the message light on my answering machine was blinking. :-)

My first phone conversation with Chase's mom was a reunion for the two of us. This was followed by more days of back and forth phone calling that finally led to definite plans. Chase and his family would come to Alexandria and we would go pontooning together. It wasn't until all arrangements were finalized that I told Brady he would be reunited with his 'old' friend Chase in just a matter of days.

On the phone, with Brady's dad back in Arizona, I told him that indeed the two childhood friends would be reunited this forthcoming weekend. He paused and said, "You're a good grandma". Hmmmm...not so sure about that! Brady had asked his 'good grandma' before and I hadn't heard what he was saying to me.

When the day of the reunion finally arrived, Joe put our pontoon on the lake where Chase's family was staying for the weekend. We crossed the water and found the house. As if we were a taxi, we pulled up next to the dock. Chase and his mom and Chase's little sister boarded with beach towels and snacks.

Chase's mom and I reunited easily...both of us excited for the day ahead.

At first the two boys sat glancing sideways at each other as the pontoon drifted from shore. I can only assume they were letting the physical changes from age 3 to age 11 sink in.

The first while was filled with talk about the *facts;*
Chase had a little sister now, so does Brady
Chase likes school, so does Brady.
Chase has a cell phone, so does Brady.

Joe and I and Chase's mom all participated in this beginning part ... then gradually the conversation split, with adults talking amongst themselves ... and Brady and Chase together.

As the pontoon floated away ... so did the seven and a half years.

Seven years had passed since they were small. Brady was usually the 'leader' in their play time together, choosing make-believe scenarios as they talked on their toy 'chatter phones'. They often picked identical riding toys during playtime outside.

But now, as grown-up 11 year olds, there was no leader. Now in the sun and the sparkling water it is companionship. Joe had inflated a water raft big enough for both guys to climb on and be pulled through the water together. Totally at ease in the lake, the two would find a rock - throw it in the lake and both go diving to find it. We all watched as they played Frisbee, jumping, hooting and splashing together. They came back on board only to eat. They were talking nonstop ... *they* were BACK!

11

When the sun was setting we delivered Chase's family back to dry land with warm goodbyes and promises.

I think Brady got what he needed from that day. What my grandson had been asking for ... was the final piece of his Minnesota picture. After they moved to Arizona, Brady still had his Minnesota grandparents and Minnesota cousins and Minnesota aunts and uncles ... the Minnesota *family* part of his life was still complete.

But the jigsaw puzzle picture of his 11-year-old life had been laying on a table ... silently ... missing one piece ... an "old" childhood friend had been missing ... until now.

Boston Legal

I spent one weekend watching an entire season of Boston Legal on DVD. I loved that show because no matter what issue was in court – it gave me a perspective of both sides of the issue…it made things not so black and white and added the shades of gray that I call compassion.

The closing of each episode of Boston Legal was always my favorite part with Alan Shore and Denny Crane sitting on the outdoor patio with cigars and drinks in hand. Here is where they talked about real life.

At the end of one such episode they were talking about a woman that Alan Shore was pursuing. Alan Shore said to Denny Crane. "I saw her laughing with another man."

Quickly leaning forward, expression aghast, at the serious implications of this discovery, Denny Crane said, "No! Are you sure? Maybe she's just having sex with him?"

"No" said Alan Shore earnestly, "No…I'm sure…she was laughing."

Laughing together … a true sign of love … something more than just sex. And it comes in all shapes and sizes regardless of the fact that the "Ken-and-Barbie-living-in-the-suburbs" image still fills the minds of many.

◆ ◆ ◆ ◆ ◆ ◆ ◆ ◆ ◆ ◆

I was alone one day checking my phone, sitting in the parking lot outside J.C. Penney at the mall in St. Cloud, MN, when I saw a couple in my rear view mirror walking to the parked car next to me.

The excess weight on the woman's thighs rippled under the nylon dress in the July heat. She was easily twice the width of the man strolling beside her. The long hair down her back could have been trimmed and shaped long ago.

Talking in an intimate way, they were oblivious to my watching.

They were holding hands as they approached the rusty blue two door car just 10 feet away. He unlocked the passenger door, smoothly pulling the backseat forward for her to deposit her lone package. As she bent slightly, the dress hitched and accented the abundant hips.

Before she could retrieve herself from the bent position, the long fingers of his hand were spread wide and cupping a plentiful handful of her derriere. He fondled the flesh with a contented comfortable stroke.

She stood to face him ... both smiling deeply into each other's eyes ... and then ... there it was ... she tossed her head back ... and she laughed!

They didn't *look* like Ken and Barbie ... they weren't *famous* like Brad and Angelina ... they weren't *royalty* like Prince William and Kate Middleton ... they were two people in love.

It was an unlikely place to see love, there in the parking lot in St Cloud, MN, but I saw it. And in that moment ... I knew ... Alan Shore and Denny Crane knew ... EXACTLY what they were talking about.

In Defense of Weakness

I thought my lifelong friend was coming to talk about the loss of her brother ... and she did. Her pain was fresh and raw. The wounds to her soul and heart were obvious to all.

But the biggest hurt of all were the friends who had relied upon her for *their* 'soft place to fall' in the past. Those people who had come to her in their time of need seeking comfort and solace and now in HER time of need, no one wanted to hear the aching in her heart. It was at this point she walked into my home. From the depths of her pain she cried, "When is it *my* turn to be weak?"

I sat and listened to the despair of loss and the disappointment of friends. I wonder if her friends realized that they didn't need answers or words, all they had to do was to sit quietly, sit in the anguish with her, listen to the agony and allow this <u>strong</u> human being her turn, her chance to be weak.

It is no small thing to let someone be weak…it is an honor. Someone is handing over to you the most delicate vulnerable part of themselves and saying, "Here, would you hold this for me for a while? I can't carry one more ounce of heartache alone. I can't take one more step without you beside me."

And when finally they are ready to pick up some of the pieces and walk out – you will hand back to them their most vulnerable self and say, "It has been an honor to hold this part of you. Come back, old friend, and be weak with me anytime."

◆◆◆◆◆◆◆◆◆

Julia and I were not friends or even acquaintances. We met in a place where weakness was the norm. There were no masks at this retreat.

Dan, the man in the wheelchair, was directing the women's workshop shortly after the death of my father. And at this retreat, I was scared of what I would find there inside myself. Moreover, Dan the man in the wheelchair, chose a random participant to play the role of my deceased father, so that I now could say all the things I needed to say. That random participant was Julia.

Julia and I sat on a carpeted floor in the middle of the room, surrounded by a circle of women. I looked into her eyes as she received the words of love, admiration, and loss that were meant for my dad. When I was 'wept out' and 'cried dry' and spoke my last word, she accepted it all in my father's stead, with tear filled eyes.

Then later that evening ... when it was over she said to me softly, "I'm jealous". I was dumbfounded as she continued, "I'm jealous that you had a dad that you loved like that". I was amazed at her ability to hear my loss, when she had no experience with loving a father as I had. She had allowed me to be weak in her arms.

Years later, an electronic message came from Julia that her mother had died.

I knew this was no time for cell phone communication. Nothing would do but face to face.

Without telling Julia I was coming, I drove the two hours on the day of the funeral. I knew she would be busy at the service with details and greeting people - that was OK with me – I just wanted to sit at the back of the church ... so she could glance back and see me there ... so that she knew I was watching ... I would catch her vulnerable part if she needed it. I wanted her to know that I remembered ... I remembered she had once carried me and let me be weak. I was here to repay the debt.

When Julia saw me at the back of the church, her entire body seemed to unwind. First a small smile crossed her face and then the tears came as she quickly approached and melted into my arms. There it was ... without a word she knew ... that now ... it was her turn to be weak.

I was thinking of how Julia must be feeling right now... I had been down this road before her. I know her path was different than mine – the landscape *has* to be different because each parent and child is unique. But when I watched Julia at the end of the ceremony descending the aisle, carrying the box with her mother's ashes, I could no longer hold back the tears. It was too ironic; the woman who had cradled Julia in her arms as a baby, was now, herself, in ashes ... in the arms of her daughter.

As Julia carried the ashes, with my eyes I said to her, "A long time ago you carried my pain for me. So, here, let me hold this agony for you for a while – I can carry the heartache with you. With me by your side, you *can* take another step. I am here ... and because I am here ... it is your turn ... to be weak..."

Country Girl

Years ago after a conference speaking engagement in Southern Minnesota I still had my hair pulled back in permed curls, Joe and I stopped by the farm of an acquaintance on our way home. I was wearing a nearly white cream-colored dress with white high heels, as we chatted with our friends. I was bursting with the question I could barely keep from blurting out, "Can we go out to the barn and see the baby pigs???"

"But" our friend stuttered, "You'll get dirty!"

I reached for a tote bag beside me and said excitedly, "It all washes! And I can change clothes!" and so I did.

◆◆◆◆◆◆◆◆◆◆

In Yankton SD visiting Joe's aunt and uncle there was a man out in the field planting corn. Hardly able to wait until the farmer eventually ran out of gas and came to the side of the field, I bolted over to the tractor and had him explain to me how the planter works … asking question after question. He too, looked at the hair and make-up as I asked if I could sit on the tractor. He said "You'll get dirty!"

I said "It all washes!" and climbed aboard.

◆ ◆ ◆ ◆ ◆ ◆ ◆ ◆ ◆ ◆

It's was my mother and father-in-law's 50th wedding anniversary, and I was again wearing a white dress, brocade this time, with puffed sleeves and white sandals – once again hair back in permed curls. I overheard some farmers talking about crops and I leaned in to hear as they talked about the price of milk. I was interested and I entered the conversation just briefly with a few comments and questions, then quickly left the to help serve food to guests.

Minutes later, the farmer approached saying, "You don't look like a farmer, but you certainly know about the price of milk ... how do you know that?"

◆ ◆ ◆ ◆ ◆ ◆ ◆ ◆ ◆ ◆

And then there was the year 2000, when our youngest son graduated from high school. My husband, of eight years, and I had been living between two places. I was at the 'house in town' where I operated a daycare and he was 'at the farm' in the country.

After eight years of married life, I had promised my husband that after our youngest graduated from high school, I would move to the country.

21

Inside I was nervous. After all, what if I didn't like living all that way from town – a *whole seven miles*!

Three weeks later, after moving to the country, I looked around at the house and the land ... the sunsets ... the quiet ... the peace ... and I wondered how I had ever lived anywhere else.

I had no idea *so much* 'country' had been lying dormant inside. When I lived in town, I had hints and nudges that the country was calling but I paid no attention whatsoever.

Now that I live in the country, there are times when I am in town at the grocery store and the sun is shining and I just want to **go home** ... to go to the country ... where comfort is available in abundance ... free for the taking ... I own the skies there ... the air is mine ... the trusted earth beneath my feet is mine ... oh, I know, all of it is just on loan to me - and *that is precisely why* I treasure it so deeply ... *it is mine now ... it is a deep part of me* ... anytime I want I can put on a dress and high heels ... but it never covers up the country girl inside.

If That Old Barn Could Talk

You remember John O'Hurley right? Sure you do! He was the guy who looked way too dignified to host a TV show like FAMILY FEUD. And sure enough, when I read his books, I saw that he _was_ made of deeper stuff than the TV show lead you to believe. In his book, John O'Hurley wishes for his children to have many 'parents' in their lives. He advised his children to make friends with people who are older and wiser and who will love them like a child … encouraging his children to 're-parent' all through life. The key, of course, is to NOT wait until _your_ parents are gone, before you start this gathering of new parents or 're-parenting' as he calls it.

Joe and I have 're-parented' through the years and, as suggested, we didn't wait until our own parents were gone to begin the process. As a matter of fact, we didn't even realize that we _were_ 're-parenting'… we simply chose people we really wanted to spend time with, and some of them happened to be a few years older than ourselves....we were doing it right! Who knew?

When we found ourselves without parents as our 20th Anniversary vow renewal approached, it was only natural to choose Don & Irene and Josie & Bill as honorary parents for our day. They were already a huge part of our lives and we were asking them to take the honored seats that in the past had belonged to our respective parents.

This year, at the end of May, our dear father figure, Don passed away ... stories from Don and Irene's history and their life together began to float to the surface as if by magic. One particular story was told over and over. Don and Irene were farming together ...both had growing children to be cared for . They were in the early years of their marriage. There was a barn that was rough and weathered and in need of paint. As the story goes, one day while Don was out in the field, on the tractor, Irene took a bucket of paint & a paint brush...and on the rough, raw and exposed boards of the barn in HUGE letters painted   **I LOVE YOU**.

As the years went by, that barn got painted...and I don't know what color that barn eventually got painted – it doesn't matter, because the original wood under the paint held on tight to the I LOVE YOU – no matter how many times that barn got painted – the I LOVE YOU held on and whispered through....nothing could hide it... nothing could white-wash it ... or red-wash it...or any other color.

I pondered these thoughts while my husband was gone on a fishing trip... I pondered that story looking at *our own* barn ... several days later I got a bucket of white paint and a brush. On a private side of the barn, I walked through the tall grass to the wall and proceeded to paint **I love you** on the side of the barn.

 But *my* I LOVE YOU felt small and immature compared to Don and Irene's...their love went through deep struggles and challenges...they worked harder...toiled longer....they earned the depth of their love, and somehow I think *their* barn knows that ...

 ... their barn knows that LOVE put those words there with emotion and hope and passion and connection...and I wonder if maybe the I LOVE YOU words just felt so good on those raw and exposed boards, like a balm or a salve, and if maybe that's WHY, why the barn held on so tight to those words ... to that thought...to that feeling ... of two people ... on a farm ... in love ... if that old barn could talk – it might tell of storms or crops or animals, but somehow I think ... that old barn would tell of a great love story... a love story that grew on sunshine and rain ... that weathered storms and droughts and bugs – a love story that their barn will embrace forever.

A Defining Moment

When I think about it I can still feel the tension in my fifth grade classroom.

My childhood was a time of reverent respect for teachers; almost in awe of them. This teacher had a stern face and was not pretty. Rarely did she get distressed. She was self-assured and had a confidence that she was good at what she did. But this particular day she was upset! She took it personally that we, the majority of the fifth graders, had tested poorly on our Weekly Reader (weekly news for grade school) exam. There were only five students out of 30 who had passed the quiz.

Everyone in the room was instructed to take out the previous week's current events flyer and reread it, preparing to retake the exam. All in the room EXCEPT for the five who had passed the test.

She ceremoniously took out her grade book to read the names of the five. We all knew with great likelihood which of the classmates had passed. There was Ralph, a vibrant good natured smart aleck who passed easily. Then there was John who was always at the top of the class. Then there was Gary who always pulled a straight A in everything. The mental list went on in my head as she began reading the names.

In the middle of the list recitation was MY name. I sat quietly listening to the information until she, the teacher, hesitated at my name and said, "Let me go back and double check that". I held my breath. Everyone was watching and waiting. I knew I was *not* considered one of the smart kids. And yet, she was checking to see if I was one of the five. And there it was...I had passed.

But her hesitation at my name was a declaration to the world that I was **not** one of the chosen ones. Not one of the ones expected to excel. Not one of the five. I was mortified! And yet I knew I had been taking the easy way out - sitting on the sidelines. I knew that I had the ability to be in that line up, but was not. I knew the teachers actions were only bearing out what I already recognized inside myself. She had not set out to hurt my feelings. She was only speaking the truth.

Now, with the ember of embarrassment burning in my mind, I had a decision to make. And there was nowhere to look except at myself. Was I going to stay on the *sideline*? It was so easy to just sit there ... and watch everything and everybody else go by.

Somehow I knew that this defining moment could go either way. It's like a boulder teetering on the edge of a cliff. That boulder can stay hanging there in place for a long time not moving or changing at all …or it can choose, with one little push, to make a big transformation. I knew I could choose to be offended or choose to take the current truth and transform it.

I chose to put just a bit of pressure on one side of that boulder and allow the momentum to carry me to an entirely new location in life.

Even now, all these years later, there is a sizzling place in my brain that remembers that sinking split second. And I am ever grateful for that teacher's straightforward and honest response. That fresh location I arrived at, is a new mindset ... a new mindset that told me I had it in me to be one of the five ... a new mindset that told me to never doubt my abilities again ... a new mindset that told me to never let anyone else fill me with uncertainty.

Why didn't *the teacher* expect me to be one of the five? Because *I didn't expect me* to be one of the five.

That changed.

Standing Alone

"Hey mom!" my college student son shouted over the phone.

"There's a big party this weekend at a friend's farm! I was wondering if I could use your van to take the guys to the party?"

A seven passenger van … my very first brand new vehicle. With less than fifty miles on the odometer and no license plates yet, the new stickers still in the window. It was a fragrant experience – the smell of NEW.

The party would be about 45 miles away and he and his friends were trying to locate a vehicle large enough for their group and the only option was my new van.

'You won't be drinking then, correct?' I asked. He assured me he would not. After asking questions and weighing the information, I agreed and did so without consulting my husband; after all, I had just purchased it myself. Why would I consult someone when I know very well the personal character of my son?

When I told my husband about the request, his response to the request did not match mine. He raised objections. Several objections actually! He was very concerned about other vehicles that might damage it or that somebody might get 'sick' in it. The question I asked my husband was "Has John ever done anything to make us doubt his level of responsibility?" We both had to admit that the answer to the question was 'NO'.

As the day of the party approached Joe was still not convinced the choice was the right one, but I handed over the keys to my nineteen-year-old without hesitation.

The word had spread through the party goers, that someone was bringing a brand new vehicle. A special parking spot was designated, way away from the general parking. All bases were covered...the driver was sober and the vehicle was out of range of other drivers. In the early morning hours, I heard John come home and go to his room.

Rising the next day John told us of the commotion at the party. All were in awe that a teenager had been entrusted with a brand new vehicle. He told of the special parking place that was set aside completely away from the other parking area so there was no chance of a bump or a scratch. When it was time to leave the party, they went to another party and stayed a short time.

John got more glories that night for the trust that was placed in his hands than he ever would have gotten holding a beer in his hand ... more praise for not drinking than all the rest.

When they were headed home; from the driver's seat John warned, "Now don't anybody throw UP!!!"

30

For John;

What does it feel like to be nineteen and handed not only the keys but the responsibility? How good does it feel to not have a drink when 199 others are all drinking? What do the other 199 learn when one young man gets more credit for standing out ... standing alone ... and standing above the crowd?

The truth is: when you have created a positive bank account filled with trust ... when you have built equity in a relationship ... you have the privilege of making a withdrawal ... he had earned it ... with a big balance left over.

The best part for me was having a nineteen-year-old that I trust implicitly ... having a son who made a statement to his friends ... and knowing ... this son is mine.

The T-Shirt

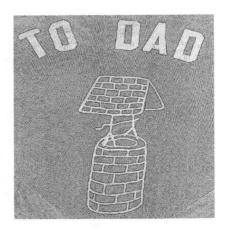

I tossed the t-shirt on the floor before my shower this morning. A half an hour later I picked it up and stopped to turn it right side out. You know how it is, you don't really look at the thing you're handling, it's just a process of picking up after yourself. But today, I felt the embroidery on the t-shirt and stopped to really look at it.

When dad was alive, he had a great habit of changing hobbies every five years or so. For about five years he used a metal detector and combed the yards of old churches and parks. He had a time when he made spoon racks and Knick knack shelves...there were the years he had a glass and collectibles business in his basement...and then there were the years he made wishing wells. And when dad made something, it was built solid to last forever. He perfected the process as he progressed, figuring out more efficient ways to get the job done.

I remember the day years ago when dad delivered *my* wishing well to the house in Alexandria where I ran my daycare ... it was one of the first he had made...thus it was *heavy* – I mean *really heavy*...he brought it in three pieces because, although dad was strong, even *he* could not handle the sheer weight. Dad never coddled himself because of a crippled arm....he was always trying new things...learning and looking for ways to improve his creations and this day, he vowed to make them weigh less!!!!

On the busy street in Alexandria, people often stared and asked about it. I wanted to thank dad for the magnificent wishing well that drew constant comments from passers-by. This of course was before the day of screen printing and electronic embroidery and simply going on the internet to create something personalized. So I set about finding someone in town to create the t-shirt you see above. As the years went by I would see him wearing it occasionally around the house...I doubt he ever wore it in public.

Through the years of its life in town, I scraped and painted the wood and the heavy metal crossbar and occasionally we took it apart and moved it to various locations. I have pictures of the boys as they grew up next to the wishing well and a photo of me in a white ruffled wedding gown shortly before I took dad's arm, as Joe and I were married.

The wishing well has been with me longer than my children have been with me.

After dad died, and after I closed my daycare in town, we gently brought the old wishing well to our country home … Joe wanted to rebuild it and I emphatically declined…dad is gone and the wishing well will rest peacefully, under my watchful eye, under a canopy of trees, here in the country as I see it every day.

After dad died…I got the t-shirt back and it's been at the bottom of a stack of clothing. Somehow, a few days ago, I grabbed this t-shirt while searching for something soft to wear. And this morning, just a few days before Christmas I stopped…felt the fabric…looked out the window at the wishing well… as the tears rolled down my face. And I wonder…I wonder if somehow dad knew, that 13 years after he was gone, I would be standing here looking out and missing him as much today as I did 13 years ago.

As I gaze at the wishing-well out my window I think "If I could have one wish right now, I would wish that I could sit with him and talk one more time…feel those enormous arms of love…and put my hand in his."

Three Sons, One Room

Yesterday I talked to granddaughter Maggie on the phone. She told me that she slept in her mom and dad's room last night.

"Why?' I asked.

In a casual, almost sing song matter-of-fact tone she stated, "Because my brother was gone to a birthday party for the night".

"I see" I said.

And, as a matter of fact … I did see.

My mind went back to the old four bedroom house on Fillmore Street when the boys were small. The creek of the old wooden steps going upstairs was just a normal part of everyday life.

It was normal to hear basketballs bouncing and baseballs falling with a thud out of a glove. We had three small bedrooms upstairs. The floors in those rooms were old cracked linoleum that had the design worn down to black in the walkways. Those floors were cold and drafty and everyone needed slippers after a bath before bed.

Even though there were three bedrooms, one for each son.

Even though each room had comfortable beds and pillows and blankets and stuffed animals and toys and games.

Even though the boys bellowed at each other to "Get out of my room!" during the daytime or "Don't touch my stuff!" … when bedtime came Rob and Tom would drag their blankets and pillows to John's room.

John climbed into the top bunk and his brothers would crawl into the bottom bunk, one at each end.

I never questioned it … that's the way it felt best.

I decided to buy carpeting for John's room. The boys and I picked out an inexpensive carpet. Although I had planned to ask a friend to install it, I had recently met a man named Joe :-) (who would years later become my forever partner) … and he offered to lay the carpet.

Joe helped us haul it upstairs and we moved the bunk beds and dresser out of the room. It didn't take long to roll it out and cut it to fit. We vacuumed up the scraps of carpet and put the furniture back.

Being involved in the busy work, I stopped to glance over at John and saw the expression on his face. I saw what he saw. The old linoleum was gone and the whole room had magically transformed into an inviting comfortable space. He came to me with the camera to capture the moment. It had never occurred to me how much carpet would change the feel of this room that was once cold.

Why had I chosen to put a soft floor in John's room first? Because John's room was the boys' gathering place each night at bedtime … now with softness and warmth Rob and Tom, as usual, would drag their blankets and pillows to John's room. Now they could choose the lower bunk or a space on the floor.

This was their time of comfort. I have no idea what they talked about or thought about. But I know that, just like Maggie, they felt close and safe knowing their brothers were near. And they are still that way… always knowing their brothers are there for them.

I know that if I could … just one more time … I would love to be that mom sitting downstairs … knowing that my three sons were all in one room upstairs … talking together or being quiet together.

And I think that if they could …
                    … they would like to do it again too.

Misha's Arms

A little girl shorter than my dining room table came toddling through my daycare one day. I watched her walk right under the dining room table with plenty of clearance!

I'd seen lots of head bumps under this piece of furniture but this was a first! So petite was she, that she walked right under the table. She had fine curly auburn hair, big round eyes and itty bitty peg teeth. This adorable little peanut walked all around the room, under the table and into my arms and heart that day.

I told myself that she couldn't possibly know what had just happened ... that she was too small to be aware that her mother had suddenly died. She couldn't know the course of her life had changed forever ... or could she? Why wouldn't she crawl into her father's arms for comfort right now? Could she feel the grief that burned inside of him?

Was she really just a little girl who knew nothing of what was going on?

As the days, weeks and months passed, I told her every day, whether she understood the words or not, "Even though your mom's not here right now, she loves you very much." Me? I was honored...honored that in a teeny tiny way I was able to 'mother' her.

With little Misha by my side, the weeks and years rolled by.

Years later, with little daycare munchkins playing at my feet, I knew I was facing a decision ... my dad was ill. I had to be by his side. I knew that there was no amount of money that could comfort me if I was not in the place I needed to be by my dad's side. And so ... one day I closed my daycare ... my children were suddenly gone to someone else's house. I don't know what the parents told their children; my reason for closing.

Five months later, I called little Misha's grandmother to tell her that my dad had died. Her grandmother encouraged me to stop at preschool to see Misha. I hesitated. Should I stop to see a, now, five-year-old? And yet, her grandmother 's words were tugging at my heart strings. She urged me a second time to stop and see Misha at preschool. She thought I should tell Misha that my dad had died. Still, I hesitated.

Finally, on my way out of town to make funeral arrangements, I pulled into the preschool parking lot.

I entered the preschool classroom and scanned the miniature tables of kids coloring, until my eyes met hers. The depth of sadness in Misha's eyes flooded over me. She *knew* … I don't how she KNEW … she KNEW everything … she KNEW exactly how I was feeling – she knew the depth of the loss. Only five years old and yet how could she know? She was so small all those years ago when her mother died, – no child could possibly comprehend, I was certain…but she *does* know.

Without saying a word she rose from her desk and came to me.

I crouched down and those two little arms reached around my neck with complete understanding, as she and I melded together. Not a word was spoken as she and I cried together for a long time. Not one single word was spoken between the two of us. All of the other little people in the room were completely silent as minutes went by and I finally let her go.

When I closed my daycare how could I have known that five months later it would be the two little arms of a five year old that would comfort me beyond words? Our hearts had bonded when she lost her mother years earlier and now *she* was comforting *me* when I lost my father. Call it what you will … but the depth of her sympathy surpassed all others.

John's 13th Christmas

He was not demanding at all, just *hoping* he was considered old enough to have a stereo in his room. John was thirteen and had a stereo on his wish list for Christmas.

The previous few years John had worked hard by my side at daycare; we spent those years paying off bills …and he knew it…that made it much easier to convince him that a stereo was completely out of the question. I promised him some clothes and a new pair of tennis shoes for Christmas. The discussion of stereos ended as quickly as it began.

Joe and I started shopping and looking at stereo ads. I had decided on a certain style at a certain price but I didn't buy it. I didn't want the big box in the house. Someone might guess what was in it. So, I waited … not realizing that in our small town when supplies run out … there is no refilling them before Christmas. So here it was two days before the holiday and no stereo for John. I was in frenzy.

As Joe left for St. Cloud on Christmas Eve day I told him "Do NOT come back without a stereo. I don't care what it costs, there *has* to be a stereo under the tree."

Upon his return, Joe went unnoticed as he took the huge box directly to the basement through the outside access door. There was very little wrapping paper left … just bits and pieces … so I took different colors of paper and newspaper and taped them all together until the pieces covered the entire surface. It was an ugly package, that's for sure!

That Christmas Eve night Joe put it under the tree shortly before it was time to open gifts. My mom and dad had arrived for dinner. Few questions were asked about the big box. No one was particularly curious - it was so dreadfully wrapped.

With mom and dad watching, John opened his tennis shoes and already had them on his feet.

The gift opening continued until the only package left was the ugly one. I finally slid the big box across the floor and simply said, "Merry Christmas John."

With total surprise on his face he said; "This is for me?"

Ripping paper and tape off the box, he finally revealed its contents. For seconds, there was a total hush.

"A stereo!" he said as he sat down in a chair next to the box in shock.

Then, he stood up "A stereo!" he said again.

Then he sat down and again said, "A stereo!"

Moments of disbelief passed until finally, still dumbfounded my thirteen-year-old was in my arms ... head on my shoulder and tears falling from both of our eyes.

My mom and dad sat side-by-side on the piano bench with their heads hung low and eyes staring at the floor, not wanting to intrude on this moment.

I'm so glad they were here, because the stereo had nothing at all to do with what was really happening. The stereo was a rite of passage. All the bills that we had paid off were not just *my* accomplishment in those years – they were John's as well ... his assistance with my work and his willing attitude was irreplaceable. He deserved that stereo...he deserved to be an adult ... he had earned it.

I wanted mom and dad to experience with us how much our life had been blessed – I wanted them to share our massive gift of love this year. Love in a box ... it just came disguised as a stereo.

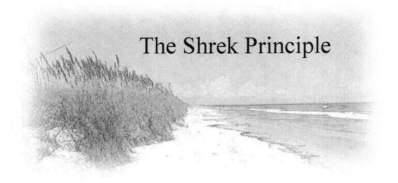

The Shrek Principle

I'm sure I was the oldest person in the room. This group of high school and first year technical students were lively at dinner. I was seated at a table with an advisor on my left and a high school senior named Adam on my right.

I could feel my nervousness as I stepped to the platform to present The Shrek Principle. I was beginning to relax when I realized that nearly all of them had, indeed, seen the movie. Princess Fiona's graceful acceptance of her unconventional beauty as an ogre, pulled them easily into the self-esteem topic.

Normally, I never use the word 'God' in my speaking or writing … not because I don't believe in God, but rather, because I don't want to alienate anyone in the audience. However, this particular night, I used a story where God could not be deleted.

The story … was about a young boy in Tennessee many years ago. He and his mother carried a stigma in that era, because the boy had no father. The boy would go to church on Sundays but always left before the service ended and the congregation was released. He feared being taunted once again by the townspeople asking him the dreaded question, "Who's your daddy?" To which the boy had no reply.

One particular Sunday a new minister was lecturing. The little boy, engrossed in the message, forgot to leave early. As the crowd dispersed, his attempt to escape quietly was met with disaster. The young boy came face to face with the robes of the new minister. Without thinking, the minister asked, "Who are you, boy? Who's your daddy?"

Instantly realizing the boys' embarrassment, the minister turned to the fatherless young man and said, "Oh, I should have known … why the resemblance is remarkable … of course … you … you are a child of God."

The young boy was Ben Hooper … who went on to become the governor of the state of Tennessee. The governors life experience shows the power of reframing; and choosing what we focus on. I went on to ask the students, "What do you choose to focus on … the negative or the positive experiences in life?"

In the entire presentation, this was the only reference to God.

As I finished and sat down I was thrilled to have connected with this adolescent group. I quietly slid back into my chair at the table as the program continued. Almost inaudibly Adam, the high school senior, leaned over and whispered, "Are you a Christian?"

Surprised by his question I simply replied, "Yes".

"I thought so" he said.

Then ... leaning toward me once more ... quietly he whispered ... "God bless you"...

The Nudge

The birthday gathering was for our youngest son Tommy. It was a backyard barbeque or, more accurately, a barbeque taking place on a friend's deck. Tom's friends were all around and Joe and I were invited too, on this warm August night.

I was sitting on an old small metal chair, just watching all the activity and I thought I was inconspicuous as I leaned back in the chair up against the frame of the deck, watching and listening to the friends of my son. The young group chided and laughed out loud together, as food cooked on the grill.

I was taken by surprise when a beautiful young girl, who was soon to be a bride, looked at me and said "I loved your book!" She said, "Tom kept asking me 'How many times have you cried so far?' and I didn't want to tell him how often I cried". Then almost in a whisper she said, only to me, "I just loved your book."

And there it was...this young single girl without children, crashing my preconception to pieces. I didn't think someone her age would like my book - I didn't think she would have the maturity to see the value of the small monumental moments that are the building blocks of life...

Then my son chimed in. "A gal that works at my office went in the back room every time there was a break in customers, so she could sit and read it! She loved it too!" Tom said, "She kept asking me "Do you remember this event? Did you cry when you read it?""

Young people all around were discussing my book, Travels on the Yellow Brick Road; Lessons Learned on the Path to Oz. Is this a miracle? To me it was. Was it a nudge prodding me … to motivate me … to keep going. To keep putting moments such as *this very moment* on paper ... a way to carry some of our stories along the timeline of life? The stories that become a trail of thoughts and impressions that shape and build an existence.

Every family has them, if only we could put them in one place in our mind and then pull one out when we need them most. Paper is the next best thing.

Oh, I know, life isn't perfect. I know that not every experience is wonderful! But life is a heck of a lot more perfect than we give it credit for ... the painful things hang around way too long ... sometimes the good things are way too short-lived.

I want to keep the good stuff handy and within reach at all times ... it makes life ... so much brighter.

Playing Hooky

He is the center of our galaxy, I'll admit that.

Brady had been asking for two days to go carp spearing again. The stars aligned one afternoon and all three of us were free at the same time. Joe and I and 12-year-old Brady loaded up the trusty old Ford pick-up truck. The three of us squished together in the cab ready to play for the afternoon.

Me? I was a spectator, armed with a digital camera for capturing the moment ... not the fish.

Arriving at the culvert on this cool July afternoon, the smell of decaying fish was strong. Someone had been taking carp from the water and leaving them on the bank to rot. The odor did not deter a twelve year old. Joe made sure both he and Brady were armed with equipment as they made their way down the bank to the water.

In the sparkling cold stream stood a young boy, perhaps 8 years old, with a very sober expression on his face. I glanced at his socks and shoes neatly sitting on the shore. All alone he was using what *used to be* a spear ... now it was just the tines from a spear...no handle at all ... just a metal shaft in hand as he attempted to capture fish at very close range! I felt bad for this determined Huckleberry Finn chasing fish with no handle on his spear and I wished we had brought extra equipment.

Brady and Joe descended the hill into the water. Carp were darting between rocks, fighting to get upstream. In short order our five gallon bucket was being filled.

From the water Brady hollered "Come on in Grandma Cathy!" "You can do this Grandma Cathy!"

Camera in hand, I declined several times, but after the third invitation I agreed to enter the cold flow of water...refreshing?!? Joe handed me his spear and stepped back to watch grandma and grandson having a ball, while little Huck Finn kept trying to stab a fish.

Immediately the sound of the rushing water was lulling and I almost missed Brady's softly spoken words, "Would you like to use mine?" Brady asked the boy.

Huck Finn said "Huh?"

"You wanna use mine?" Brady said again to the younger boy.

There was an emphatic vigorous nod of the head from Huck as Brady handed over his spear. The two of them swapped back and forth – one shagging the fish in the direction of the other – one with the spear and then vice versa ... if Joe and I were not spearing then they both had a whole spear ... all the while telling each other "There's one behind you!" "There's one in the rocks!" "There's a BIG one over there!"

Returning to sit on the culvert, alone with the sound of rushing water, I put the camera away ... it couldn't capture what was being recorded on my heart. I saw something that afternoon about Brady's soul, about his core, about his true self ... and my heart wept ...

Where does world peace begin? Right here ... right now ... in the moment of knowing that we are not separate in the stream.

Pearl

Sometimes it's lonely when your parents are gone; it's a feeling of not being anchored. Those two people who, no matter what, were watching out for you, and sometimes now it feels solitary. Those two people were always on your side. It was one of those days and I was feeling small and ordinary and alone in the world.

I was chopping vegetables at the kitchen counter for supper when the phone rang that day. A woman's deep voice said, "Cathy?"

I said "Yes"

She said "Hi this is Pearl!"

Surprised I said, "Well Pearl! So nice to hear from you! It's been years!" I welcomed the voice from the past. Pearl was now in assisted living and occasionally I would stop to visit and listen to her play the piano and sing for the other residents. She also had been a toastmaster, and I had the opportunity to hear her speak.

"Say Cathy" she said, "I had my daughter go and pick up a copy of your book for me".

"Oh good", I said

She said "I couldn't stop reading it ... it was phenomenal!" I thanked her.

She said "You know my daughter heard you speak a couple years back. She said you were wonderful. And then I saw the article in the newspaper six months ago about your book. So I asked her to get me a copy."

As if she knew I needed her; she said in her natural deep tone of voice, "I just wanted you to know ... I'm watching you."

I got off the phone and stood silently over the vegetables, letting the feelings and thoughts sink into my heart and brain.

"She's watching me..." I repeated over and over in my mind as I cried onto the vegetables I was chopping. "She's watching me..." How did she know I needed a parents arm that day? It felt so good to know that someone on earth is 'keeping an eye on me'. Someone who didn't just think about me, but physically picked up the phone and called to tell me they noticed. That phone call was one of the most powerful I have ever received ... it is what I call a 'God Thing'. I needed it and the Universe said to Pearl. "Pearl, call Cathy!" ... and Pearl listened and picked up the phone and called me.

I hope I pick up the phone when I'm nudged to call someone ... because I would like to be the one delivering the feeling that Pearl delivered to me today.

Maggie's Handwriting

On the phone with Maggie one evening she told me she and her mom had sent Joe and I a thank you card in a purple envelope. I asked her what the card said. She said, "It says thank you for the table and chairs."

When it was finally delivered into my hands I found Maggie's card and envelope *inside* of the larger Thank You card from her mom and dad.

I was stunned to see the advances our little Maggie had made in printing the letters of the alphabet. All of the letters were easily readable and well formed.   I was stunned! There it was – time passing while Maggie is growing up and learning …

I tried several times to get Maggie on the phone – it was a busy weekend and no one was answering ... finally I sent a text message to Maggie's daddy – and five minutes later my home phone rang.

Now, a normal conversation with Maggie at this age, consists of Maggie doing about 75% of the talking, but this time was MY turn.

I told her I got her card and she asked, "What did it say? I can't remember."

So I said "Hold on while I get it – because you see I have already put your card in my SAVE FOREVER folder – do you know what that means?" "No" she replied. "That means that this card is SO special and precious to me that I put it in a file to KEEP IT FOREVER – never to throw it away. OK, now I have it"

I said to her "It says 'Thank you for the table and chairs Bye Maggie' and the front of the envelope says Grandma Cathy."

"But Maggie," I said "I have something else I want to tell you".

"What?" she said.

In a soft serious voice I said –"Maggie when I opened your letter, I couldn't believe how beautiful your hand writing is... (I can hear Maggie quietly breathing into the phone) all of the letters are so perfect...(intent listening silence) ...I didn't know you had learned so much since the I saw you last ..."

"Oh" she said almost inaudibly.

I continued "... and when we come to Arizona in December, I want you to sit down with me and let me *watch* you write..."(long silent pause) slowly, seriously and quietly she said 'OK we can do that"... finally I said tenderly, "Thank you for my card Maggie".

"You're welcome" she said kindly.

After we got off the phone I smiled ... I knew I had made a big deal of her improved handwriting. I want Maggie to know that I'm watching her ... that I'm paying close attention ... that I notice and care about the small and the big things ... more importantly, I want her to *assume* grandma cares ... cares about the purple envelope ... cares about her handwriting ... and cares about *every single step she takes*.

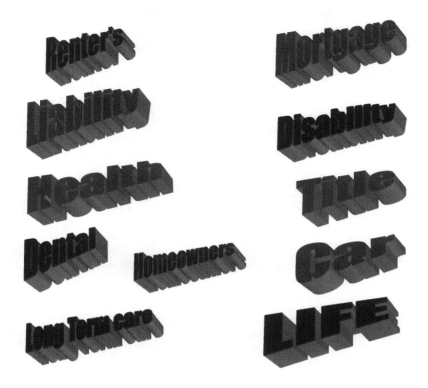

Some day I'd like to walk into an insurance agency and say, "I'd like a Whole Life Happiness policy please! I'll pay *any* amount of money that it takes. You see, I want assurance that on the day I take my last breath, I will have
1) lived my hearts' desire and
2) that every interaction with others would be uplifting."

I want insurance to guarantee that the things I say will be taken *the way it was intended.*

If I say hurtful things ... I want a high deductible ... to be forgiven and have the wrong be automatically substituted with right.

I want insurance that will assure I think positively about myself and others.

I want an agreement that declares I will care more about the person standing right next to me than those our country has alienated by war.

I want a declaration that leads me to draw on the strengths I already possess ... but don't use.

I want an assurance of the heart – coverage for a full and satisfying life.

"Oh" the agent might say, "we can't possibly do *that*!"

"Why not?" I would ask. "I'm willing to pay any price! Your ad says you offer 'peace -of- mind'

"I'm sorry" he would say, " all we can replace are the *things you own.*" The things you are asking for come from the heart. They are priceless."

Ah yes, in my imagination I think ... as I see myself walking out of his office, it's crystal clear. They replace the trinkets we have – they cannot replace our most prized possessions ... the part of us that is truly priceless ... the part that fills life with meaning ... our connection to family, friends and humanity ...

Next time, in my imaginary conversation, I'm going to ask for hair insurance ... so I'll never have a bad hair day again ... I bet there's no insurance for that either ...

The Fabric Store

She was trying to look at the colors and weights of the fabric. Two little boys were yanking at her legs, begging to go ... to see the puppies at the pet store just across the mall. They couldn't go alone and so the pleading continued as she shopped. I could tell that the mother was getting agitated. I could see it on her face. I knew the feeling well ... once upon a time ... a long time ago.

They talk ceaselessly, these two little men as they prodded her. "What are you looking for?" one asked. "Why do you need this?" Then the other, unrelenting, asked, "Can we go now?"

A moment later came a great exclamation from the older little boy. His big little voice said, "Oh! This is BEAUTY-full!"

Curious to see what had captured his excitement, I turned and saw him holding a piece of bright orange checkered fabric with a high gloss finish. One word described the fabric; obnoxious. But his enthusiasm convinced me, that to him, it was nothing less than remarkable.

I said to the woman, "Oh, his expression is soooooo precious!" She looked at me with tired eyes and simply nodded.

She and her sons continued through the fabric store toward the mall entrance while I strolled through the store. As I scanned the calicos ... I found tears welling up in my eyes. I knew what her sons were saying to her. They were saying; 'You'll have lots of time for browsing in a fabric store when we're grown up ... for right now ... watch us grow ... let's play! '

But I couldn't tell her what they were saying - for right now her life is heavy with responsibility ... and juggling ... and trying to get everything done ... I have been there too. I couldn't tell her to just STOP ... sit down ... and gaze into the eyes of these children who will soon be in their own cars ... gone to play elsewhere.

Now ... I shop, uninterrupted, with memories of little boys by my side.

There are times my jeans catch on something ... and for just a moment ... I feel the tug ... I feel the love attached to a little hand ... sons who used a pull on my leg ... now pull on my heart. The warmth of a little hand in mine ... will always remain.

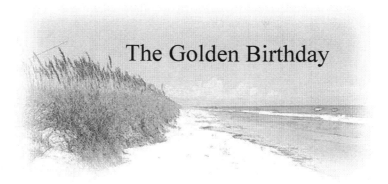

The Golden Birthday

His golden birthday was being celebrated at a bar – like the TV show CHEERS! That kind of bar with everyone calling "Norm!" and where 'everybody knows your name' – a place where the crowd keeps growing all night long and all of them are friends of the golden child – 29 years old on the 29th of August.

Rob had been helping Joe and me with remodeling our house every free weekend that was available to him, so we had been hearing for weeks about the upcoming party...and it was going to be no surprise that ALL for Rob's large group of friends would "be there or be square."

None of the parents were invited ... it didn't matter – even with sheet rock and extension cords everywhere around me, there was nothing that was going to keep me from at least making an appearance at this milestone birthday party two hours away. Of course I didn't tell Rob we were coming.

With construction dust on every surface in our house and no spare time to bake a cake, I ran to the store and bought two boxes of Rice Krispies and three bags of marshmallows on the morning of Rob's birthday. Hurriedly

I melted the marshmallows in the microwave with two sticks of butter to make them extra good gooey! After they cooled, I stacked the bars in a pyramid and added 29 blue candles.

Two hours later, as we neared the freeway exit where the birthday party was being held, Joe called Rob on his cell phone to wish him a happy birthday.

Ten minutes after the phone call to Rob, we were in the parking lot hoping Rob wouldn't see us from the window, but the party was actually located on the back deck outside, so there was no way for him to catch a glimpse of us. To our astonishment we parked next to … drum roll … Rob's dad! His intention was the same as ours. Rob's dad was waiting in the parking lot for a friend of his to arrive, so Joe and I were the first parents to enter.

Walking through the doors and scanning for Rob – he turned toward the two of us and did a double take – I mean a REAL double take – shock and surprise was total! I set the Rice Krispy Bar "Cake" down on the bar-height table and put my arms around this child of mine – he was near tears – his tight embrace and the sound of his voice told me so. "Hi Momma, I can't believe you're here," he muttered into my neck. Without letting go I said "I wouldn't have missed this for the world!"

Rob proceeded to introduce us to all his friends as his 'parents'.

Ten minutes later; Rob's dad and his girlfriend walked in. Now Rob had some backtracking to do and had to explain that Joe was actually his step-dad.

An hour later; the 'parent circus' became even more hilarious when Rob's ex-stepmother and her boyfriend walked in! And another round of parent introductions took place – none of it was preplanned or prearranged – <u>none of the parents had even been invited</u> ... SIX, count them, SIX parents.

As the party grew ... and grew ... and grew throughout the night, there was open astonishment on the part of Rob's friends, as they routinely were introduced to three sets of parents who all enjoy each other ... and three sets of parents ... who all love Robbie.

Could I Have This Dance?

With money in hand, I approached the girl at the pull-tab booth. "What are the people at that table celebrating? Is it their anniversary?" I asked, glancing toward the long table filled with mostly boisterous characters. The loud music was covering up this unusually early burst of partying.

"No" said the lady behind the counter. "It's that woman's 80th birthday."

Joe and I had noticed the decorated cake on the table amid the gathering. My eyes landed on the silver haired birthday girl in her dazzling black dress. She was tapping the tabletop to the sound of ♪"You Ain't Nothin' but a Hound Dog" ♪ coming from the stage. She and her partner were seated across from one another at the end of the long table nearest the dance floor.

Joe and I watched the family celebration from the sidelines, enjoying it as much as the live band. From time to time their middle aged 'kids' filled the center of the dance floor while the older couple floated around the outside laughing at the grown children's antics. ... and yet somehow these two were alone amid the party.

He would gallantly offer his hand to her and ask if she wanted to dance. It was obvious he adored her. His dazzling smile and unending attention to the lady on his arm was the stuff fairy tales are made of.

We watched and smiled at them as they floated across the floor – occasionally dusting their shoes to glide more easily…but in fact they looked like a disk on an air hockey table, just floating on a cushion of air.

She attempted a new step with him on the edge of the dance floor. Unable to master it, she simply shrugged her shoulders as he smiled down at her. He graciously draped an arm around her shoulders, telling her without words, that the new step was unnecessary. They sat for a song or two, but no longer. Within minutes his hand was offered for the next dance. It was clear this couple knew how to pace themselves…so they could enjoy the whole night…the whole dance …

Not-so-much for the middle aged 'kids'!

10:30 PM saw the first reluctant early departure of middle-aged 'kids' heading out the door.

Half an hour later another 'kid' was partied out.

I turned to Joe and laughing out loud said, "Mark my words! When this night is over, it's going to be you and me and the 80 year olds still dancing!"

Sure enough … 1 AM arrived … the band stopped playing; the lights were coming up as Joe and I strolled over to meet the lady with the milestone birthday at the abandoned table. Now, just the two of them were seated at the long table. They had been smiling at us all night and we, at them. It was time to meet.

They welcomed us eagerly as we approached, graciously offering us chairs right next to them. We laughed together about the early departures of their 'children' and then listened intently to their tale.

These two had known each other decades ago in high school. He left to serve our country in WWII. She met a man, married, and eventually had eight children. When he came home from the war, he also married and had children. Eleven years ago now, her husband had passed away and ten years ago his wife passed away … and now here they are…dancing.

We had assumed they were married … because they dance flawlessly together with an easy knowing flow.

They had assumed we were not married … because, they said, we looked like sweethearts.

Joe and I have shared the dance floor with these two many times since that momentous 80th birthday night. That first night, looking at the two of them, I thought it was romance … a love story … and I see now that I was wrong. It's deeper than a fairy tale romance … it's camaraderie … a sharing of loss that has created something more weighty than romance … they honor each other's previously spoken vows … they had meant their former vows, they had lived their former vows and they honor each other's' past …

And Joe and I? We are privileged to be in their presence – to share the floor with them in hopes that we might … just maybe someday… have depth like that.

And so they dance … and we dance …

A Dream

Happiness was the topic on the radio as Joe worked in his shop one night.

Shortly before bedtime, we sat talking and he was telling me about money and happiness and how, according to the expert on the radio, winning the lottery ruins people's lives. The expert said that if the person winning the lottery COULD handle the responsibility, then the people around the winner could NOT. The expert said that vehicles don't make us happy. These were the thoughts rolling through his mind as he fell asleep.

"I had a really *really* nice dream last night!" Joe said the next morning.

He continued; "Some burglars broke into a house. They were typical burglars searching for money or coins or even better; gold! "

The burglars found a BIG safe. When they opened the safe, they saw something very unfamiliar; something unique and complexly original. It was intriguing actually.   Inside the safe they found a large tool box with nine transparent compartments. Each compartment had a *different* and *separate* locking system. One compartment had a padlock.

Another had a simple key lock. Another had a standard combination number lock. *Eight of the nine compartments had visible locking systems.*

It was quite obvious that each box, within the toolbox, belonged to a different individual. One box had neatly folded legal looking documents … another box had jewelry that was simply thrown in a pile haphazardly with little care or concern…another box held old coins, some of them from decades ago when the government first began putting currency sets together. Next to the currency sets, was a velvet bag with a draw string and the bag looked about half full. You knew there were probably half dollars or silver dollars in the bag, because the edges of the coins pressed outward on the velvet revealing the shape of coins.

Another box had velvet jewelry cases all neatly lined up in a row, all of them with closed covers. This was an ingenious creation allowing nine different people to have a safe-within-a-safe.

The oddity was, of course, was the ninth box. The ninth box at the very bottom, had no visible locking system and was filled with bars of gold.

The burglars were not at all intrigued with the eight boxes that had typical securing schemes. The obvious locks on the eight boxes, the burglars had seen before. There was nothing challenging or even interesting about them. The easy answer would be to take the money and jewels from the "easy-open" variety lock boxes and get out.

But the burglars were not satisfied with smaller quantities. They wanted the BIG win – the BIG prize - the gold bars.

The two kept working and trying to get into the cubicle filled with gold bars, all the while completely ignoring the eight "easy-open" containers. Diligently they continued to work on the completely sealed cubicle filled with gold bars ... but their time was up, the authorities were upon them ... at the very same time ... they realized ... that the gold bars were fake ... everything else in the safe was real."

Astonished at his dream story, I said, "That is a great story"!

I can't wait to find out what's on the radio tonight!

Movie Night

Andrea and I are buds. I mean deep down rock bottom explorers of inner life. Always dissecting and searching through thoughts and motivations until it's all a pile of mush and yes - yes, we have scrounged a few morsels of learning and we will file it away for safe keeping.

We mash and grind through social motivation and spiritual levels, cascading our way to matters of the individual heart. My time with Andrea is a roller-coaster ride of laughter and serious talk and total enjoyment.

And this is precisely why we ended up *locked in an empty movie theatre.*

Our carousel conversation began *before* arriving at the movie. Then of course, the movie itself, triggered new topics of conversation as the credits rolled.

Without missing a beat we resumed our conversation as other movie goers left us.   We knew that when the second nightly showing started, we would decide whether to watch it again or move on to another location to continue our discussion. And so we talked in the darkened theatre ... and talked ... and talked.

Until finally, we realized that no one was entering; no second show was beginning. This movie theater has 9 different movies showing each night. This movie, the one we saw, must not have sold any tickets for the second show, but certainly, the other eight movies were already well into their second showing for the night. I was thinking about getting my free refill of popcorn before I went home, as we followed the aisle runner lights and stepped out of our theater into the lobby. All was dark except for the soft a glow of exit signs. My first thought; I wonder if there's any popcorn left?

Soon came the dawning realization that we were the only two people in the entire building. Our eyes locked, realizing everything was completely shut down. My heart quickened just a bit as thoughts began entering my brain. In the glow of the dim exit signs the question running through my mind was, "How the heck did this happen?"

I asked Andrea "How the heck are we going to get out of here? If we open a door to let ourselves out, it's going to set off an alarm."

My new cell phone had arrived in a box in the mail that day and it was at home charging for the very first time. So Andrea used her cell phone to call the police. She told them that we were inside the closed movie theatre and we were about to open a door, which would set off the alarm.

The police said to wait and they would send a car over and so we stood inside the darkened movie theatre waiting. As we stood by the door, not daring to open it, two police cars drove up from two different directions. We stepped out of the theatre and, indeed, an alarm started buzzing.

I sighed with relief when I recognized one of the police officers. I stepped out of the door and said, "Hi Kevin!" and gave him a big hug. "So sorry to inconvenience you". We explained what happened and thanked them for coming so quickly.

What movie did we see? Who knows!

All I know is that it created a great conversation between Andrea and I once again. And the situation created a great memory for two lifelong friends; being locked in a movie theatre, totally unaware of the world, because the conversation was so engaging, we couldn't have cared less what was going on in the world around us.

That ... is a friend. *That* ... is someone you would *want to be* locked up alone with. Someone so likeable ... so interesting ... so thought provoking ... that a whole boatload of popcorn sitting under a warming light ... could go completely unnoticed.

A Fairy Tale Moment

I never cry at weddings. Why cry? I love watching people play Cinderella and Prince Charming! I think everyone should be able to live the fairytale for a day without anyone mentioning that 'reality' is waiting in the next tomorrow.

This day my husband and I are escorting his eighty-year-old father to a wedding where he will be giving away the bride, his granddaughter.

For weeks, residents at his senior complex have been buzzing about this upcoming event ... waiting for the moment. After all, how often is someone who lives in a retirement complex asked to be part of a wedding party?

Stepping out of his apartment in a black tuxedo, my father-in-law is using a walker. A beautiful black cane will replace this piece of equipment for the ceremonial stroll down the aisle.

I have set aside extra film in the camera of my mind and heart for today. I want to indelibly print a picture in my

73

brain of the way Joe's dad looks right now ... the pride ... the excitement ... it would have been so precious if his wife of 53 years were here to share the moment. She would be fussing with his bow tie and removing microscopic pieces of lint or hair from his tuxedo. But alas, his bride is waiting for him in the next place.

It will be more than an hour before the ceremony begins. This quiet church nestled in the woods should quiet my non-stop activity level. Never have I experienced a more peaceful and serene setting for a house of worship – they should all be like this – the nature of God's earth touching each soul.

In spite of the setting, my internal throttle was not idling down to the tranquility that surrounded me.

I watched the groom beaming – the bride blushing. The photographer was taking his time placing each participant in the appropriate place for the perfect pictures.

Near the altar, of this country church, is a woman practicing a song. She is a strong, solidly built woman with a wonderful voice.

With nothing but time on my hands while the photographer continued his work, I strolled over to the woman and introduced myself. It turns out she is the mother of the groom. They are farm people – comfortable people. I comment on her voice and how precious that she is singing at her son's wedding. She told me she had written this song. I was surprised ... because the strength in her hands spoke only of hard work – these hands didn't show any time for something frivolous.

She said, "It's kind of funny the way it came to be written". Her eyes took on a faraway look as she pictured in her mind every detail of the story she was about to tell. My attention was now fully in her hands. Although I was standing, I mentally eased back in my chair for the telling.

She described a time and a season that reminded me of a song. The lyrics go, "... you picked a fine time to leave me Lucille ... with four hungry children and the crops in the field". No, she wasn't leaving the relationship, but indeed, she was leaving for a few days to fulfill an obligation. She had promised to deliver a friend's belongings to her new home, three states away. In spite of her husband asking her to reconsider during this demanding time of harvest, she had to keep this commitment.

Taking the horse trailer and a truck, she and *another* friend loaded up the furnishings and headed across the great, long open, state of North Dakota.

Half way through the trip, out in the middle of nowhere ... the truck broke down.

At this point in the telling, my heart sank ... since the friend who was relocating had preceded them, I surmised that the only option available was to call her harvesting husband for help.

She called her husband back home and told him they were stranded. This man ... stopped the machinery ... drove to the middle of nowhere ... picked them up ... hooked onto the trailer ... journeyed with them to their destination ... traveled all the way back home with his wife ... not once speaking a word of reprimand. It was on this trip home – hours in the vehicle ... she sits writing a song of love ... the one she will be singing today at her son's wedding in less than an hour...

I glanced at her husband across the room. I pictured this country man ... with his bride broken down in an obscure location ... I know that it was an easy choice – not easy to leave behind his responsibility – but easy to decide where he belonged. In a heartbeat the decision had been made.

I found myself wondering if I could ever ... be that good? ... be that understanding? ... have that much empathy?

With this story tucked away in my head, I was escorted by a young tuxedoed man to a seat a few rows from the front of the church. I slid to the end of the bench to get a full view of my husband's dad as he escorted the bride to the altar. A fairy tale moment was about to unfold.

The mother of the groom sang beautifully. As the piece of music flowed, her eyes were on her husband and no other. The words drifted melodically off the top of her voice. ♫"He's my love, my friend, on him I do depend
        I thank you Lord for giving him to me." ♫

The lyrics had a destination and the rest of us were outsiders watching as they floated to her husband in the front row. With eyes locked, I knew that heaven and earth could have fallen away and neither one of them would have noticed.

I was moved ... if the whole assemblage had known what I knew about this song, they would have been crying too ... weeping over a love story that took place on a farm … in a truck … with a horse trailer ... half way across the country ... at harvest time.

The final blow that burst my floodgates came when her husband, at the front of the church, offered his prayer for the newly united couple. His wish for them was to love Christ first. Then ... locking eyes with his wife ... looking only at her ... he wished the couple a love as deep as the love he and his wife share. In that fairytale moment, there was no one else in their world ... a private moment in a public place.

"You picked a fine time to leave me Lucille?"

Maybe Lucille needed ... just once ... to feel more important than the crops in the field.

A Hero in a Truck

I didn't see the child...I didn't see anything at all except a Plumbing and Heating truck at a complete stop in the busy street. The truck was a good distance from the crosswalk on the other side. I stopped ... because he stopped. Checking the crosswalk between the two parks, I saw no one. I stayed stopped...because he stayed stopped. Traffic was backing up behind me from my direction and behind him from his direction.

A gasp caught in my throat when I finally saw what he saw.

As if in slow motion I saw a child, a little boy, appearing not yet to be three years old, smiling and unaware of danger. Running playfully onto the roadway the little boy could have easily reached out and touched the grillwork on the truck.

The man in the truck watched as a frantic mother raced into the street toward her child. The child, enjoying the game, merrily ran the other way – toward the middle of the street.

The man *in* the truck was now *out* of his truck, like a linebacker with his feet planted and arms spread.

The little boy was quickly surveying his options ... his mother on one side...an imposing linebacker blocking his path on the other. The choice was easy. The little guy went rushing to his protector...the arms of his mother.

I exhaled as the mother and child reunion took place and the man got back into his truck.

Turning the corner onto 10th Ave. my eyes clouded with tears.

There is a young mother today who has the privilege of taking her child home ... whole ... and intact.

There is a boy ... able to grow up.

There is a man who will rest well tonight ... knowing that today ... he saved the life a child.

Then there are the rest of us ... the ones who witnessed an enormous act of kindness and community. The statement "It takes a whole community to raise (and protect) a child" means more to me today than it did yesterday.

Zephyr Ride

My dad was like a kid in a candy store as we entered the train station. I could see the memories flooding through his mind, from the days when his father would let him ride in the train engineer's car. The train, in the small town of Morton, MN, had been a regular part of my dad's life.

My dad was a boy during the Great Depression when so many had lost jobs and everything they had worked for. My dad's dad, my grandpa, worked for the railroad and had hoped he would be one of the few able to keep their job during the depression. But in the end he was not. My dad would say, with a far off look in his eye that this was the only day he ever saw his father cry. The day his father came home without a job during the Great Depression. That's when my grandpa started farming.

Everyone carries the stories and beliefs created by their circumstance and my dad was no exception. Some of the fear of those financial times could not help but carry forward into the rest of my dad's life.

80

◆◆◆◆◆◆◆◆◆◆

The dinner tickets for today were paid for in advance and if my dad had known how much the tickets cost for the Zephyr Train Ride adventure we were about to take, it would have spoiled the day of fun for him.

So here we are in Stillwater, MN, in a time of plenty, stepping into a railroad depot. My dad was giddy with excitement as he looked at the memorabilia on the walls of the depot and began telling stories from his childhood, most of which I had never heard before.

This was a dinner train, not a train to transport either people or cargo to any destination at all.

Stepping into a train car of luxury we were escorted to our table by a waiter dressed in black dress pants and a vest with a bow tie and white starched shirt. Our cocktails arrived before the train even began to move.

There were female singers on the train wearing WWII period uniforms going from table to table. They sang ♫"Boogie Woogie Bugle Boy of Company B".♫ Dad grinned so wide I thought his face would never go back to its original shape. Dad's grin always attracted those ladies to our table…they leaned in close near him and sang a song by the Andrews Sisters ♫ "Don't sit under the apple tree, with anyone else but me".♫

We traveled for fifteen miles that day on the train and it took three and a half hours, returning to the exact same place that we had departed from. The entire time dining on

81

a five course meal and dessert so beautiful one didn't want to cut into it.

When the slow peaceful ride was over I paid cash for the drinks and tip. I saw my dad glancing at the cash in my hand and I know he thought this was covering the price of the entire daytrip.

This excursion was one of the greatest joys of my life. Years earlier, when I had no extra money, I remember thinking to myself about all of the things I would give to others if only I had the money. I vowed that someday I would be able to give … and here it was … I was receiving more joy from this day ... watching my dad ... than my heart could hold.

Grizzly Adams at Wal Mart
December 28th 2005

Three days after Christmas, I stepped into the check-out lane at the grocery store.

The checker monotonously asked the same question of everyone, "How was your Christmas?" And the expected answer was, "Good, really good." So the checker asked the man ahead of me the obligatory question. "How was your Christmas?"

The man ahead of me was burly ... I mean BURLY and BIG around. Backwoods type in striped bib overalls that stretched over a BIG belly. He had a mass of shoulder length curly graying hair. The front tooth that was missing was nearly concealed by long graying whiskers. The beard and hair melded together allowing other people to see only his eyes and nose. I expected a huge voice to come out of a body this size but instead he quietly said, "Well, this was the _best Christmas I ever had!"_

The checker behind the counter said nothing. Nothing! I couldn't believe it! Somebody says they had the best Christmas they _ever_ had and no one asks why!!!!

Looking at this heavy-duty farmhand type man in bib overalls, I said "Well, *I've gotta ask*! *WHY* was this the best Christmas you've ever had?"

He turned to me gratefully with an enormous smile and said, "My grandson was born!!!! Can't you see me, I'm *still* flying high !?!" And indeed, I could.

The excitement in his voice was rising as the words almost stumbled over each other trying to get out of his mouth. He said "Now, this baby...*this* baby has a set of lungs on him! Ooohh yes! My son...when he was born...never cried...no siree! He was always quiet, but *this* one...this one can really holler! And his hair is just like his daddy's was when he was born... and real long fingers too..." He gestured inches beyond his own labor stained calloused fingertips.

I just watched him as he left the store ... felt the excitement that will never go away ... I know because I live with grandchildren in my heart every day, with every breath I take. Where do those grandparent hopes, dreams and tears come from?

It's my theory that all the years of loving our own kids, accumulates over time ... and as it accumulates ... it distills and becomes concentrated like fragrance oils ... and it's there inside, just waiting for the right time to use it – it ages and becomes a richer aroma with every passing day – and then *that* day comes – the *one* day when a child is born ... and this farmer/backwoods man ... instantly and immediately becomes a grandfather. No pretense.

In my mind's eye I was looking off into the future. I could see this heavily built man moving his beard aside and laying a newborn baby gently on his chest. And that baby... sleeping long and full of peace as the big belly lifts and lowers... absorbing that fragrance of grandfather love. That love will make the calloused large fingers become tender as they touch the soft new white skin ... and the bearded man will ponder which year he will wear a Santa suit ... and all the while he ponders that thought, the baby is breathing in and breathing out ... becoming accustomed to the scent of grandfather love. The little boy will always remember the scent of that love ... as grandfather and grandson nap ... in the enormous arms of love.

Happy Anniversary

My mind was groggy with sleep as the 6 AM alarm was beeping – but I had been awake for a while thinking about the day ahead and realizing that this day would have been my mom and dad's wedding anniversary if they were still with us.

I turned on my Thai Chi DVD and was about to do a quick check of my email Inbox before exercising. This message is what I found:

" OK Cathy. Seven months after you handed me a copy of <u>Travels on the Yellow Brick Road</u>, and amid my own travels looking for the 'all powerful Oz', I find myself inextricably placed in your life. Page 20, I am already breaking down my own walls, finding a tear of appreciation. As real people, we are so blessed to understand that in the end, we each have nothing beyond our relationships, and the stories behind and around them. Thank you. Only on page 21, but already, thank you and blessyou.

Lotsoflove,
Alan,Karen,andSabrina
Brownsville, TX "

As I read this note from a kindred soul I wondered *what story he was talking about!?!* Page 20 and 21? I had written the book nearly a decade ago now and had no idea what story had solicited this response. In the quiet dark morning, I grabbed a tattered copy of Travels on the Yellow Brick Road and sat to read while the exercise DVD continued without me. This is what I found;

A Donut Afternoon

Each afternoon my mom and dad drove to the bakery in Cold Spring, MN. They bought a roll and coffee...then parked by Super Valu...ate their treats...and watched people come and go.

In the hustle of my busy young life, I silently scoffed at their routine. My perception of their afternoons falls into the category of being a time waster.

I looked at it differently when I saw them become frustrated with their inability to transport themselves after dad got sick. They no longer could shop for their own necessities – to enjoy the simple pleasure of travelling together...just the two of them.

I watched mom cry one afternoon as dad laid in the living room in his hospital bed. All she wanted was an afternoon drive together ...to get a donut...with my dad. A simple request that was impossible to fulfill...any one of the kids could have taken them where they wanted to go, but it wouldn't have been the same.

If they argued about medical decisions I thought it was signs of weakness in their relationship...what a fool I was... I thought I knew so much about people and life.

Their disagreements had nothing at all to do with the underlying foundation…there was a bond between the two of them that couldn't be broken if the powers of heaven and hell came together.

Mom had ceaseless energy caring for dad…many hours a day…nights without sleep…the demands…how did she find the strength? I asked her one day. Shrugging her shoulders she stated with unequivocal certainty, "Well…I know he'd do it for me."

The donut afternoon was a comfortable part of their day…two people together…they often didn't talk about anything…now I realize…mom and dad were talking all the time…I just couldn't hear it.

◆ ◆ ◆ ◆ ◆ ◆ ◆ ◆ ◆

I sat on the sofa stunned that I had been directed by an email ... to THIS story ... on THIS day ... mom and dad's wedding anniversary.

Just Buying Eggs

It was snowing on my first day in Cottonwood, Arizona. Out loud, all by myself in the car, I was shrieking, "Are you kidding me? I am in Arizona for crying out loud!!!" This must be some kind of joke. I know how to drive in Minnesota snow with an all-wheel drive vehicle but...c'mon!!! I'm driving a CAR!!!!!

In the area West of Sedona, I'm all by myself, not knowing anyone who lives here and driving switchbacks to hypnosis training class early in the morning and then back again each night.

Did I mention class? Oh yes, even that I kept asking myself, "Why am I here?" ' I don't HAVE to do this and yet this path has been calling me for a long time. "I'm such a coward," I say to myself! So what if I'm a thousand miles from home? So what if I'm driving in the mountains in snow? At least in Arizona every flake is melting as soon as it hits the ground!

I'm whining, I know I am, and as I write I wish that my words would somehow flow like the words of Elizabeth Gilbert when she said "I am here, showing up to do my part and if maybe some unnamed divine entity may pass

through to help me – that would be great right about now!"
Shoot, not feeling any divine help at all.

But the divine moment did come eventually.

Day after day of studying and I was still wondering if the
time and the money and the determination will be worth it.
I laughed out loud my first day entering Cornville, AZ.
Really, who thought of that name? That's a name for Iowa!
Turning to the right, I see along the roadside a mini-ranch
with fences and chickens and a barn…and a sign by the
road EGGS FOR SALE.

Oh my, I LOVE eggs and I promise myself that I will stop
to buy some eggs that evening. By the time class was over
the sign was gone! Rats! I watched the next day too and no
sign. Day 4 on my way to class there was the sign again.
Today I promise myself that when lunch time comes;
buying eggs is going to be my destination.

Days of intense training and still I am carrying self-doubts
in a knap sack on my back like a hiker through a forest
wondering if there will ever be a clearing in this damned
forest.

At lunchtime I got in my car and drove to the EGGS FOR
SALE place. It was a mini ranch with a white washed gate
fences across the driveway. The sun was shining
magnificently as I walked across the yard. Doors and
windows were open in the house with the Arizona fresh air
flowing through. As I looked for someone who might sell
me some eggs, there were chickens clucking around my
ankles. I walked into the back yard to see a most adorable
red barn with a blonde haired beautiful lady walking out. I
stared at her in amazement. She was so pretty I glanced

around to see if there were cameras filming for some kind of commercial for healthy skin.

I said "I'd like to buy some eggs. Three dozen if you have that many."

After exchanging names, she asked "Where is your accent from?"

"Minnesota" I replied.

"What are you doing in Arizona?" she asked

"I'm studying clinical hypnosis". In Minnesota that statement would have caused the listener to pause, scowl and question my sanity. In this woman, there was no sign that this was anything out of the ordinary.

"When is your birthday?" she asked immediately.

I told her my birthday, although I thought it an odd question.

Matter-of-factly, without missing a beat, she looked directly into my eyes and said, "You will transform & rejuvenate people's lives on a one-on-one basis. You are now living your life by DESIGN".

Stunned doesn't begin to describe the feeling I had inside as I walked back to the car. Getting into the rental car I swear I was floating on the seat ... instantly ... the heavy knapsack of doubt ... slid off my shoulders.

I looked up her name later on the internet and found ...Debbie Crick; internationally renowned expert on the **Cards of Illumination Inc.**

Goals

When my three boys were little, I was a single mom and I decided that we needed to set some goals and pay some bills. We paid off small bills first and then moved on to pay off the vehicle that we had at the time.

Of course I included my three little boys in the accomplishment of these goals. So every time we had an extra $10.00 or an extra $20.00 we would go to the bank and make an extra payment. It got to the point that the tellers at the bank knew whose boys these were and so I would often just park in the lot and send one of the boys in to make the extra payment on our vehicle.

After a long period of time, the day finally came when we got to make the last payment on the van. Of course I took my three little boys along to the bank ... now remember this was a time when $5.00 was more than they could spend ... I can assure you that is not the case now!

So I had my three little boys sit in the lounge chairs at the center of the bank while I went to the teller window to make the final payment.

I returned with $45.00 in $5.00 bills. I crouched down to their level and I put three 5 dollar bills in each one of their laps. They sat there with eyes as wide as saucers! I said to them "This is for you to spend on anything that you would like, because you have worked hard to accomplish this goal."

They stared at me with eyes filled with wonder! Each grasped their money tightly as we headed for the outer doors. There was a stunned silence between the three of them that was louder than anything I had ever heard. We were just at the door ... just ready to step outside ... when my oldest son John ... turned to his two younger brothers and said. "I can't *wait* till we pay off the *house*!"

Whoa!

Wikipedia says of Jim Klobuchar; James John "Jim" Klobuchar (born April 9, 1928) is a Minnesota journalist, author, and travel guide. He wrote for the Star Tribune in Minneapolis for three decades, and now writes an occasional column for the Christian Science Monitor. He is father of U.S. Senator Amy Klobuchar.

◆◆◆◆◆◆◆◆◆◆

In 2013 I sat listening to Jim Klobuchar give the keynote address in the small town of Sauk Centre Minnesota. The annual writer's conference is held there each year in honor of author Sinclair Lewis who grew up there and wrote about Sauk Center.

Klobuchar's personal story was riveting. He took us with him through the ups and downs of his life both on a personal level as well as writing. His experience and history of reporting election returns caught my attention ...typing on a manual typewriter ... sending AP bulletins election results from Minnesota each paragraph - one at a time - being yanked out of the typewriter and a 'runner' who literally ran to a teletype ...until all five paragraphs had individually been sent to the world ... everyone waiting for Minnesota... made me realize that this man's writing had developed right along with technology and history...one step at a time.

He continued speaking calmly, and candidly laying out his years of writing in chronological order and none of us in the audience were recognizing that a monumental point in his life story was about to be set before us, like a glorious desert on a silver platter at the end of a meal.

Casually, almost off handedly, he said that one day he had been out of the office and upon returning someone said to him, "I sure wish you had been in your office today!"

'Why?" he asked.

"Because Ernest Hemingway is at the Mayo Clinic and he's been reading the Star Tribune. He called and asked to speak to you. When you weren't in he said, "Tell him I like the way he writes."

The audience sat in total complete dumbfounded silence...

... it seemed like the air went out of the room ...

... then without warning a soft voice from the crowd said a long drawn out "Whooooaaa!"

Two lone hands began to applaud ... slowly ... amid the reverential silence. The applause spread like 'the wave' at a baseball stadium through the audience.

What ... a ... compliment.

I will never forget the chills that ran down my spine at that second ... a man's entire life spent writing ... and Ernest Hemingway called. Whoa!

What's For Supper Honey?

Elmer was ahead of his time. Joe's dad was in the salvage business *way* before anyone else saw the need. Most people didn't understand his work. It would take years for this awareness to blossom within our town and in society as a whole. As soon as he retired from his job, his part-time recycling operation went into full-time mode.

This morning Elmer is in a worn thin, almost see-through, cotton shirt with the sleeves deliberately torn out. He takes the two front shirt tails – one in each hand and ties them into a knot accenting his belly. To complete the morning ensemble, he puts on a flannel shirt over the top to ward off the early morning crisp air.

What lies before him is a day of hard work, a day of salvage. There is more work ahead of him than one man or even ten can accomplish in a reasonable amount of time. He will be taking apart discarded once-useful items, to recover reusable parts and recyclable metals. There is no way for him to keep up with all that gets thrown away.

His wife, Ruth, is petite and gray; she rarely leaves the house, unless hitching a ride to a grocery store. After 50 years of living together with this man, she knows that this day will be the same as many others. She will go about her tasks just as he does his.

Before leaving the house to begin the day, Elmer leans down toward this extremely short woman and in the quiet tone of private intimacy and he asks, "What are we having for supper tonight honey?"

With their two heads tipped together she quietly explains that they have a leftover ham in the refrigerator which she plans to make into boiled dinner with cabbage. He nods a satisfied look to her, then straightens to full height, as he readies himself for the day ahead.

What was this that I just witnessed? It was an exchange of only a few words and a couple of sentences. But ... this was not the first time I'd heard him ask that question of her. As a matter of fact it was not the second time either. So today when I heard it again ... I paid attention.

I watched the interaction between these two people who have been together for decades and finally I realized he routinely, perhaps on a daily basis, asks this question as he's leaving the house. This meal prepared by her hands is his motivation ... his reward at the end of a hard day's work. Yet it was a closeness ... saying to each other that our nearness will be tonight after we both have worked hard – then we will sit side by side, sometimes quiet, sometimes not ... but always by each other's side. It is the comfort of day-after-dayness in their lives.

◆◆◆◆◆◆◆◆◆

97

Those two adorable people are gone now... the salvage yard is gone ... and there is no ham in my refrigerator ... and yet there are times when my husband is going to work out in his shop and I hear him ask; "What are we having for supper tonight honey?"

As I reply ... the echoes of his dearly departed parents warm my heart and I smile ...

Uncle Jim's Wisdom

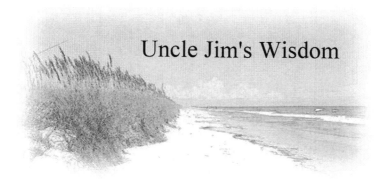

I get to hear from my Uncle Jim almost every day! Well, it's not JUST for me, but he sends out a group Humor email that began as a daily gift to his friends who are homebound. Each Humor letter starts out with his personal 'thoughts for the day'. Often times he will talk about the damned squirrels that harass his flowers and yard or what he has been planting and of course, he talks about the good food they eat at restaurants in East Texas. The following was one such opening;

"Good morning from Stephens Lane, all is well here.

I'm not sure what others would've done had they known they wouldn't be here for the tomorrow that we all take for granted. I think they would have called family members and a few close friends. They might have called a few former friends to apologize and mend fences for past squabbles. I like to think they would have gone out for a Chinese dinner or for whatever their favorite food was.

I'm guessing; I'll never know what they would have done and that is OK with me because it is the things I have left undone that matter. It's those little things that I left undone that would make me angry if I knew my hours were limited. Angry because I hadn't written certain letters that I intended to write one of these days. Angry and sorry that I didn't tell my loved ones and friends often enough how much I truly love them.

I'm trying very hard not to put off, hold back, or save anything that would add laughter and luster to their lives. And every morning when I open my eyes, I try to tell myself that today is special. Every day, every minute, every breath truly is a gift from God. "People say true friends must always hold hands, but true friends don't need to hold hands because they know the other hand will always be there." Life may not be the party we hoped for, but while we are here we might as well dance."

I love that man.

Small Town America

I came to a stop at the intersection along with the rest of the busy Christmas shoppers.

There was an elderly woman crossing the street. She was in the crosswalk. She was doing everything right. However, the slow methodical penguin like steps she was taking was at a monumentally slow pace. I sat there watching and thinking, "She is never going to make it across the street before the light changes" And indeed she did <u>not</u>.

Across the intersection was a huge city snow removal truck waiting to make a left hand turn and all other lanes of traffic were filled as well. I sat with rapt attention to see if any of the drivers would make a right hand turn in front of her or honk or gesture.

All was quiet…not a single vehicle moved.

The light changed and still … no one moved.

I swear you could hear the collective sigh, as she finally, painstakingly, took the last step off the street onto the sidewalk.

As I drove away I said out loud "God (really meaning God!) I love small town America!"

The Monument

What could possibly be so urgent that this business man left a message on my cell phone as well as my home phone? Deep in grief after the passing of my parents, I knew there was *nothing* this businessman could need or say or want, that warranted the urgency in his voice. After so recently losing Mom and Dad I figured there wasn't anything he could say that would rattle my cage.

The business man is from the monument company not far from mom and dad's house. My sister and I had made decisions for a headstone. In a 'normal' situation they request written approval from all family members, in case there is fighting or disharmony.

Back on that particular day, my sister and I sat looking at the books of ready-made art – thousands of pictures at our fingertips. All we had to do was decide – sounds hard and complicated but it wasn't – a tractor for dad's corner of the stone and a sewing machine for mom's corner of the stone.

Through the course of months we became known as 'the family that gets along'. Seriously, most families are disagreeing about the monument? Really?

So what could it possibly be that the man with the monument needed? We had chosen a beautiful dark granite stone – about two feet tall – they would engrave all of the information – some on the back and some on the front – everything exactly the way we had asked.

When I returned his call, I could hear the stress in his voice – perhaps it is more accurate to call it strain. He said in rapid words, "The delivery was not allowed to go forward! The area of the cemetery where your mom and dad's ashes are buried is for in-ground flat stones only! The men with the stone and the truck and the concrete were turned away! Unable to place the stone!" said the excited gentleman on the other end of the line.

When he told me the men were not allowed to put the headstone up, I started laughing and laughing until the howls were bringing tears to my eyes. The man on the phone was dumbfounded – his anxiety and nervousness and stress changed to curiosity. I heard him say to someone else in his office "She's laughing!"

He said to me now, "You're laughing!" sounding bewildered.

He continued, "In all my years this has never happened before! We need to talk to the cemetery board! We need to get an attorney!" He rambled on and continued along this vein. Finally, he quieted when he had run out of thoughts and ideas as possible solutions to the dilemma.

Quietly, very quietly, I said to him "Why don't we cut the stone right down the middle like a hamburger bun and then lay both pieces in the ground?"

Silence…dead silence on the other end of the phone.

Slowly he said, 'Well, I never thought of that!"

And now, my mom and dad have the most unique grave marker of anyone I know. The tombstone, set flat in the ground in concrete, covers the entire plot perfectly.

I chose the gravesite over the phone. The woman said that since we only needed one plot for two sets of ashes, she had a single available. In my grief and loss I paid absolutely no attention to the location and told her we would take it. When my family arrived at the cemetery we found my mom and dad's grave … right next to Grandma and Grandpa …

Three Little Angels
Hangin' On A Tree

The Angel Tree program asks you to take an angel ornament home with the name of a child on it along with a modest Christmas wish list. Each child's list includes one article of **clothing** they would like and one **toy** they might want – listing several alternate options.

My son has told me that when his adorable wife, Shannon, plucks an ornament from the Salvation Army tree each year, not just the two required items will be purchased for the angel child, but rather *all* of the items will be provided. (Lucky little angel that gets picked by Shannon!)

Rotary and Salvation Army join forces at Christmas time to distribute food and gifts *on the same day, at the same location*: a huge Phoenix parking lot. On the appointed Saturday, my son, John was a part of this well-oiled volunteer machine.

Amid the chaos of cars and trucks a woman arrived with her three children, all four on bicycles. They all had backpacks and were hoping to take their windfalls home using this mode of transportation. But whoever had plucked these three angel names off the tree was equally as generous as our dear Shannon.

John stood there looking at the food & packages, then back to the bicycles & backpacks and knew there was NO WAY it was going to fit. The thought of arranging boxes and packages on bikes was abandoned. The mother said they didn't have a car, so she and the three children had ridden their bikes four miles from their house to the pick-up spot. Now what would they do?

"Tell ya what," John said "if you give us your address...in a couple of hours, when we're done here, we'll bring your food & packages to your home." So the family departed, empty handed, to ride the four miles back home.

Several hours later John and a fellow volunteer arrived at the address the mother had provided. In the front yard was an abandoned rusted out car with four flat tires. Approaching the front door there was the sound of feet rapidly pounding down a set of stairs with high pitched children's screams, "THE PRESENTS ARE HERE! THE PRESENTS ARE HERE!"

Then came the mothers' authoritative voice above the rest saying, "Go back upstairs! You *have* to go upstairs! You can't see them, they're not *wrapped* yet!" Then was heard the much softer and slower sound of reluctant feet retreating back up the stairs.

As he told me the story my son's voice was low and quiet on the phone. He said, "Ya know Mom, there were people picking up food & gifts and this would be a PART of their Christmas ... but for *this* family ... what we delivered today was their ENTIRE Christmas".

106

The magnitude of his concluding statement sat in the silence between us.

John said, "Sometimes there are greater things at work, than we're aware of."

The Swill Cart

"I think I'm buying something for you – wanna ride along?" Joe casually asked as he walked past the front door with garden tools in hand.

I tucked my hair up under my hat and took a glance in the mirror – pretty shabby, but perfect for a ride in the old faithful Ford truck on a sunny Saturday afternoon.

After a fifteen minute drive we knocked at the door of an elderly lady. She teasingly said to Joe, "I thought this was going to be a *surprise* for your wife?"

"Oh," Joe said, "She doesn't know *what* we're here to look at!"

The woman's eyes twinkled as she led us to the back yard. Parked there in the yard was my gift ... a dilapidated swill cart. Two large wagon wheels with a free moving platform connecting them - a push handle like an extra-large baby carriage. Long ago the platform kept buckets level when they were filled with slop for the pigs. I could imagine this cart in my yard overflowing with cascading flowers – I was thrilled!

The next afternoon I called the ONLY person alive, who *would and could share my excitement...my aunt Eileen.* She was the original hard working farm woman.

I told her about the swill cart adventure the day before – and she laughed – and laughed – delighted with my excitement! Her memories, words and feelings flowed as she commenced to weave a story for me.

"Years ago", she began " when the kids were little, we were having a feud with the neighbors on the farm next to us...I have no idea what it was about...and it doesn't matter anyway."

"Well, one day" she continued, "I was driving home from town and I saw these neighbors in their driveway. They must have ordered a load of gravel delivered to be spread on their driveway, but they had no tractors or equipment to haul and spread the gravel. So the neighbors were shoveling gravel from a huge pile into five-gallon buckets by hand, lifting them onto a swill cart and pushing the cart the length of the driveway, gruelingly dumping and spreading the gravel bucket by bucket."

Eileen continued, "I went home and told Ray (her husband) to take a tractor and loader over there and help them spread that gravel! He did ... and it got to be late in the afternoon and I had to do chores by myself ... well that was no big deal! I suppose our son Terry was only about 5 years old at the time and he was worried that his dad was so late. He wanted to know if I thought maybe the neighbors had SHOT his dad! I told him 'I'm sure he's fine'. Well, it was *way* past dark when Ray finally got home and Ray said the neighbors were so appreciative they just *wouldn't* let him go! He said they fed him supper and talked and talked...he just *couldn't* get away!"

Then quietly Eileen said, "From that day on, the friendship lasted the rest of our lives. The woman just passed away a couple months ago".

I was quiet on my end of the phone, letting the magnitude of the story settle in. Where a feud had once existed – a bridge had been built.

◆ ◆ ◆ ◆ ◆ ◆ ◆ ◆ ◆ ◆

Eileen is gone now too...I feel sorry for myself when I pick up the phone and then remember that she's not there anymore. Aunt Eileen could do it for me every time. She could bring LIFE right down to the core ... get rid of all the weeds and show you exactly what is significant right there, right at the root of the matter.

She added meaning to my soul ... to my life ... and to my swill cart.

When Maggie Was Seven

The tomato/cucumber salad is bright and beautiful in the cut glass bowl – we are in the abundant sunshine and growth season. I know that when we get tired of the red and green combinations it will undoubtedly come to a grinding halt. I will preserve some tomatoes by stewing and freezing them and another season will vanish... until next year's harvest.

As I set the salad in the refrigerator the phone rings...it is 7 year old Maggie saying loudly without preamble "Wanna color!?!"

Without hesitation I say, "Yes, of course!"

When I tell people that Maggie and I color together over the phone, I get the strangest looks. People assume we use a video cam or Skype. However, 7 year old Maggie needs to move a lot when she's on the phone. She likes to wander the house saying to me, "Can you hang on a minute? I have to get a snack out of the cupboard."

And I do.

A moment later she says, "Can you hang on a minute?" and informs me that she has to go to the bathroom, which I already know, because I can hear the toilet flush. That's OK by me, I like it that way. I like the feel of being a routine part of her life, even though we are half a continent apart.

Then it's my turn to say, "Can you hang on a minute while I get my headset?" and we both chatter as we get our identical color books & markers & colors and soon the time arrives when she and I BOTH finally sit still...and color together over the phone.

She chooses the page and decides very thoughtfully exactly what color the giraffe will be.

In my adult mind I have to stretch outside the box to color the giraffe PINK, and the sky GREEN… but I do. Often times we spend 45 minutes coloring and chatting. Then, we use our smart phones to take a picture of our art work and text the photo to each other. We evaluate our coloring for this session and she tells me "you did a good job!" and I tell her "your picture is marvelous!"

One afternoon as we colored, Maggie told me "My mom is home, but my dad's not done with work yet." So we colored and chatted … and chatted and colored.

A second time she stated, "My Dad's not done with work yet" as we talked & colored.

Five minutes later she told me a *third* time, "My dad's not home yet".

With the page nearly complete she blurts out, "MY DAD'S HOME! BYE!" and the line went dead.

I LAUGHED OUT LOUD with no one to hear! I know that all is right with the world when a daughter screams, "My dad's home!" and runs to meet him.

Next season my vegetables will once again grow in the garden ... it will all come around again ...but I know that each age and stage with Maggie will not.

I know that the time is coming when I won't hear "Wanna color?" being called in my ear as I answer the phone. I know she won't always have time to chat without time constraints ... she will have sports in her life ... and school ... and sometime soon there will be teenage friends and boys.

So, for now, I hoard my time with my darling duckling Maggie, like a miser ... saving her little chatter ... smiling all the while, as I do my very best to preserve these memories ... saving them as best I can ... sometimes in words on paper ... sometimes in pages of coloring ... and always ... absolutely always ... irrevocably ... in my heart.

Smart Maggie

Joe asked me to stop by the store and pick up some Play Doh.

"Play Doh?" I asked

"Yes," he said "I have to figure out the right size bolt for my car and I need something to make an impression of the space."

So at Target, the only Play Doh I could find was in a package of four different colors. I decided that whichever colors he did <u>not use</u>, I would take the others along to Arizona for Maggie and I play with.

Later that night Maggie called to color together over the phone. With our phones on speaker, I said "Maggie! Guess what I bought for Grandpa Joe today?" "What?" she asked. "Play Doh!" I said excitedly!

I explained to her what Joe was using it for and heard my son in the background say, "That Grandpa Joe is a smart guy!" I told Maggie I would bring the unopened containers of Play Doh to Arizona for her on my next trip to visit.

We continued to chat and color when Maggie heard Joe come into the house. She immediately asked "Grandpa Joe, what color Play Doh did you use? Did you use the pink?" Joe answered, "No Maggie I didn't use the pink I used the blue, but it didn't work very well – it was too soft "

Without hesitation ... Maggie innocently ... and matter-of-factly said, "Just put it in the fridge ... "

Standing beside me Joe rolled his eyes in the expression of ***"Dah! Why didn't I think of that!"***

Joe put the PlayDoh in the refrigerator and it worked perfectly.

Happy Endings

Some people called him Rick – some people called him Rich – I always called him Richard – he would cringe and say, "That's what my mom called me when she knew I had done something wrong!" Whatever name we use, this Thanksgiving we are grateful for all the years of having had him as our neighborhood friend and country hermit ...

After Richard's passing it was Joe's responsibility to find homes for the lame, crippled and damaged animals that Richard cared for diligently. We were thrilled when the female chickens were relocated to a good home...and the pigeons were caged and taken to a new location and then ... there were the beautiful roosters ... all majestic colors of shiny black and deep gold and majestic red... some of the prettiest birds we had ever known awaiting slaughter. Richard had told us himself before he died that no one will want the roosters ...with misty eyes he told Joe "You'll have to slaughter them".

Joe kept procrastinating with the final stage of dealing with Richard's roosters...dreading the prospect of 'slaughtering' the friends who had filled the yard and life of Richard Towner.

Joe was sitting at his desk at work and turned on Swap Shop at the very end of the call-in radio program. Anyone wanting to buy or sell something can just call or email the station. One of the last calls of the day came from a couple who were looking for chickens for pets. Joe came home from work that night and told me excitedly, that he had found a home for all the roosters!

"Pets?" I said to Joe when he was telling me about the caller? "Are you kidding me? *Nobody* has old roosters for pets! That's why Richard said the roosters would have to be slaughtered!"

"I know! I know!" Joe said "but these people have animals on their farm for their grandchildren and they already have goats and horses and now they want some chickens. They want the roosters - they'll take all of them!"

Joe and I sat looking at each other in disbelief.

On the appointed evening, two warm-hearted grandparents came with grandchildren in tow...and spent the evening catching the roosters! After they took them home, they kept them in a building for the first ten days to get them acclimated to their new environment and finally let them out to roam the yard... on the phone they assured us the beautiful roosters were fine and hanging around the yard.

There were five roosters left behind; ones that were too spooked to be coaxed into cages that first night. The delightful grandparent "rescuers" came back another night to gather the final four. The fifth rooster we assume met his demise in the natural scheme of things.

Joe and I often speak in wonder about the fact that Richard took care of the details after he had crossed over ... all of his feathered friends in new caring homes.

Now ...
　　　... rest in peace Richard
　　　　　　... your work is done.

A Day with Brady

Stepping stiffly into the shower I asked myself "What in the world did I do yesterday?" I couldn't immediately identify the cause of the muscle aches through my shoulders.

And then thoughts of yesterday morning came floating into my mind and a smile of contentment automatically tagged along. Ah yes, my grandson! Just the two of us playing together.

We were berry-picking in a strawberry field at daybreak. Then we made a stop at a hotel arcade room with an air hockey table. WE BOTH play aggressively! There was laughing and hooting that instantly drew the attention of those within earshot. When we were worn out this young man asks, "What are we doing now, grandma?"

With great drama and a drum roll I announce, "Now…now I am taking you to a private tennis court!" His eyes widen and I assure him, "You and I are the only two people allowed on the court today!"

"But I've never played tennis!" he protests.

119

"Well babe," I said "Today is your day to start!"

We drove through town and I could see him considering the buildings and residences with curiosity. He was trying to predict where I would turn and I could tell that he was scanning to see a tennis court.

I put on my left turn signal entering a heavily wooded area. A question crossed his face without being spoken. Both sides of the evergreen lined driveway were lush trees that seemed to mesmerize him, with dense forest on both sides.

We bumped along the gravel rutted single lane, crossing a small bridge. Still he said nothing, just watched and looked. In a moment ... the trees parted, and as if by magic a home appeared. A green lush lawn unfolded in front of a lake sparkling perfect in the sun. And there tucked out of the way off to the right ... a tennis court!

His eyes widened in amazement as if to say, "It really IS a private tennis court!"

"Let's go meet Josie and Bill" I said enthusiastically.

My dear friend Josie wove her web of charm on my young grandson, wanting to know all about his Minnesota adventures so far. Her husband Bill was just as welcoming and got tennis shoes for Brady and balls and rackets for both of us. Ten minutes later it was just the two of us...in the sun, total novices, chasing balls and laughing ourselves silly.

Later we walked the banks of the lake together skipping stones and then sitting in the grass.

Later when I told Joe about Brady's and my morning together he said, "I'm jealous!"   And I said "You should be, it was the BEST!"

Now this morning, I step into the shower with shoulders aching, it is a most pleasant reminder of the day we had yesterday. Being with Brady not only gave us time to *play together*; it gave the adult part of me permission to not pay attention to the news … not pay attention to the outside world – not pay attention to all the things we think we need to attend to – and just BE … BE there … BE childish … BE playful … and remember that I too am a child inside.

Cinderella (8-2009)

Rob was a groomsman in another wedding ... so many good friends for him to be a part of huge monumental moments in their lives ... and me ... I had simply promised to be his driver.

Joe wasn't feeling well that evening and decided to go to bed at 11:00 PM and I changed into white jeans, a tank top, and a jean jacket. I fluffed my hair and left to chauffer my son home.

Entering the banquet room at this late hour, I saw that the reception/dance was in full swing. I found my gigantic 6 foot 4 inch son in a tuxedo. At this point the jacket had been peeled off for a night of celebrating ... and he looked great!

I met people ... lots of people, all friends and happy to include Rob's mom in the nights' festivity. One young couple on the dance floor motioned to me to come join them, so I did. Soon the DJ cleared the floor and called for only women. Ah yes! ♫ "I Knew the Bride When She Used to Rock and Roll"♫ filled the room.

Over on the side of the banquet hall was a man who looked alone and not quite as boisterous as the rest of the crowd. I know I had met him before but couldn't quite place him when Rob reminded me of his name. He and I began an intense conversation that continued for nearly 45 minutes – discussing the ups and downs of the economy and house buying and the direction his life may take, with the impending loss of his job ... so we brainstormed and talked about possibilities in a private conversation amid the noise.

Without really being aware of it, I heard the DJ say that this was the last song of the night. I was amazed at how fast the two hours had flown!

Out of the corner of my eye, I saw Rob RUNNING across the banquet room ... without breaking stride he grabbed his tuxedo jacket off the back of a chair ... a moment later he approached me with his hand outstretched ... I excused myself from the conversation and allowed this handsome young son of mine to take me to a quiet space on the dance floor. There ... he sang in my ear ♫'Wonderful Tonight'♫ from beginning to end...the whole time my eyes closed with my arms wrapped around his neck.

When the song ended and my eyes opened, cameras were going off all around the two of us. Rob's friends were shouting, "I got it! I got it!" And I thought to myself...oh no you don't...I got it! I got the best possible feeling a mom could have.

I'm sure my Fairy Godmother was hiding somewhere and watching ... and there might as well have been a horse drawn coach waiting for me outside ... I might as well have been wearing a ball gown with wide floating skirts down to the floor... I could swear I felt glass slippers on my feet too...as the two of us left the building and walked to our car in the parking lot I said, "Robbie, you always make me feel like Cinderella...always".

Mavericks

I was thrilled for John when I learned he had applied to become a member of the Mavericks; an organization of businessmen whose purpose is to raise money for various charities.

What I found most intriguing about this organization is the fact that they don't just let anyone simply choose to join. They want to keep the group to a certain size with a certain level of commitment.   John put in his application to become a member.   That particular year there were 17 applicants and only three would be chosen for membership.

A couple of weeks later while John and I were having our regularly scheduled Friday afternoon chat, I assumed that he was in his office working hard, when he said "Well, actually Mom, I'm on a golf course event with a beer in my hand enjoying the Arizona sun." He had been chosen as a member of the Mavericks.

Months later the organization was preparing for an annual event where they take young people who are facing homelessness, shopping for clothing at Kohl's department store. As the host of this event Kohl's gives all of these young people 20% off anything purchased as well as no state sales tax since it was a charitable event – yes, Arizona has tax on clothing.

During the weeks and months of preparation for this event one of the members told the new enrollees that this can be a powerful experience on both sides ... both for the member and the youth. He said that in his first experience taking a young person shopping at Kohl's, the young man had chosen jeans and a tee shirt and a couple of other items.

Since the young man had additional money available, the remainder of his $125.00 ... the man asked the boy, "What else would you like to buy?" The boy replied, "I'd like to buy a towel". The Maverick said, "Well maybe you'd rather buy another pair of jeans?"

And the young boy unquestionably said, "No ... no, I want to buy a towel". "Why do you want to buy towel?" asked the Maverick. And the boy replied, "Because we have 10 people in our house and only one towel. I want my own towel."

So he was preparing the new members for an experience ... that did come to pass ...

The next Friday afternoon when I talked to John he told me that he had been partnered with a 17-year-old young man for the shopping event. The first thing the young man wanted to look for was a pair of Van shoes...the young man's feet were a size 11 and he was currently wearing a pair of size 9 shoes. I could only imagine, as my son was telling the story, what those shoes must have looked like and felt like, full of holes and probably too tight or perhaps just plain falling apart.

So the two went and looked for a pair of Van shoes. There were two pair that interested the teenager. One pair more expensive than the other and the young man was looking at the ones that were less expensive when John told him, "You know, you're probably going to be wearing these a lot , so it might not be a bad idea to get the more expensive ones, the ones that you really like". So the young man got the better quality more expensive shoes and a pair of jeans, a tee shirt and a cap.

At this point, they had money left over out of the allotted $125.00 and John asked the 17-year-old what else he would like to buy. He said "I'd like to go back and see if I could buy the other pair of shoes, the ones that were on sale." So John and the young man went back to the shoe department, looked at the other pair of shoes that were on sale and found that there were only two pair of those left and neither one of them were size 11 .

Approaching the associate working behind the counter John asked if they could check inventory in their computer to see if by chance there was another pair of those shoes somewhere in the store. Checking the computer she said, "No ... no there was not."

Then looking down ... behind the counter ... the attendant reached for a box ... a pair of shoes that had been returned ... and there ... was a size 11 of the exact shoes he wanted that were on sale.

I could hear the 'wonder' in my son's voice as he tells the story ...'knowing' that life is not coincidence.

As they approached the checkout counter the young man became a bit anxious watching his items being totaled. He looked at John and said in an anxious tone whispered, "We forgot to figure tax." … John assured him that because it was a charity event that there was no tax on the items that they were purchasing.

As the person at the checkout counter used a tool to remove security tags from his shoes he turned to John and said a bit franticly, "What are they doing? What are they doing to my shoes?" Sounding as if they were taking something off from his shoes that he might need. And in that moment John realized that this young man had *never* purchased an item with a removable security tag.

Before leaving the store John encouraged the young man to continue with school, to get an education and a diploma. The 17-year-old said doubtfully, "But, I'm a second year senior." John replied, "Well at my son's high school graduation this last year there was a four year senior…so it doesn't matter how long it takes, don't give up!"

We receive when we give … Period … John went home with gifts that day that were much more valuable than shoes or jeans. He went home with a mountain of affirmation, that if we work hard and focus on our strengths and abilities, we can accomplish what we set out to do. He went home with the eyes of perspective … he carried with him a heart filled with compassion … and an overwhelming feeling … of being blessed.

Choking a Bird

One day when the boys were small, I was stressed out the whole day. As well as running a full time daycare, my then-husband and I had an Amway distributorship. Some of my daycare parents were routinely late picking up their kids, which in turn, made me late to pick up Amway products each Monday after work.

I tried not to let the frustration show and put a smile on my face.

One such day, while driving out of town to pick up Amway products after daycare, my four-year-old, Rob said from the back seat, "Mom, sometimes don't you just feel like climbin' a tree and choking a bird?"

I broke into peals of laughter.

I didn't realize at the time, we feel other people's stress levels in a subtle way. We think no one notices.

And a four-year-old is honest enough ... to just say it out loud.

Now when I have too much commotion packed into one day, I go back to that time and ask if I'm ready to 'climb a tree and choke a bird'

By-Invitation-Only

John's controlled and yet *excited* voice came across loud and clear into my ear on the phone. It was the voice of triumph I heard in my son's expression on the other end of the line.

The governor of the state of Arizona is going to be doing the State of the State address in the Southwest Valley of Phoenix for the first time ever! Seating is "by-invitation-only" of 200 people from across the sprawling region. From a population of 6,595,778 in the state of Arizona only 200 people would be chosen to attend...and my son was one of those 200.

He has been meeting new people and making professional friends and contacts their first year living in Phoenix. Now he had received the honor of an invitation to an experience of a lifetime. Of course I came to my computer ... created this file ... and waited in the following weeks to hear the great story that surely would be coming!

Week after week passed until I finally remembered to ask how the State of the State address was.

"I'm embarrassed to say" he said sheepishly, "I forgot to go!"

I laughed out loud! Apparently, the most important part was to be ASKED! ... to be included ... to have the choice ... and to have the chance!

◆ ◆ ◆ ◆ ◆ ◆ ◆ ◆ ◆

I can't remember when it was, that I realized that my precious friend Josie was aging. It was the awareness, there would be a time when I wouldn't have her in my life. It was <u>that</u> day several years ago; that I decided I was never going to her house without fresh baked sweet treats that she enjoyed so much.

Every week on Thursday morning there would be a plate of homemade bars or muffins or donuts sitting on the bench where my coat and purse were stored. When Joe would see the covered plate he would say, "Going to Josie's today?" But he already knew the answer.

Joe loved my weekly trip to Josie's house; for him it meant something was always baking in the oven Wednesday evening and he was the recipient too.

Josie and I worked on her memoir together...each week for years, digging through boxes of photos and papers she had saved for just this project. She and I would sit side by side at the computer, putting the puzzle pieces of her life together in pictures and words.

Years ago when we began meeting together each week, her eyes were good. As time went by, the medical appointments for her eyes increased until finally it was said out loud, that there was nothing more to be done. One day she wept as we sat together, for the loss of her eye sight. Then she entrusted me with more decisions about photos for the memoir and one time she thanked me for deleting a photo of her that I thought was not flattering to her.

I know that through the years, I had the best of Josie; I had her when her life was unhurried. I had the pleasure of knowing her intimately simply because of the project itself. We went through genealogy and stories about her parents. She talked about high school and World War II and about loving Bill. Then there were her precious children; loving them and loving Bill. Every step of her life was simply a new part of loving Bill.

This past week Josie died. I am left here at my computer screen writing without her now.

I went to the freezer this morning for meat for dinner and the first thing I saw was a container of muffins with purple sugar crystals on top. I had put them there for a time, in case I was too busy to bake on a Wednesday evening; I stood for an instant looking at the muffins knowing that there would never be another morning of writing together with Josie.

The night before my last visit with Josie, I pulled out the fry daddy and filled it with lard and turned it on to heat. With tears dripping down my cheeks I rolled out donuts. I knew it was the last time. I knew she probably couldn't eat anything. I knew I had to do it one more time ... for me ... for the two of us. Even though there is over a quarter century age difference between us, Josie and I have become sisters.

There's going to be a private funeral gathering tomorrow and it is "by-invitation-only" since the formal funeral will be held in a couple of months. I was one of the lucky ones; I received an invitation.

Now I understand why my son forgot to go to his "by-invitation-only" event. It was an accomplishment to be sure ... he had earned a spot at the event ... but that was all it was ... just an event ... there was no heart connection.

My "by-invitation-only" is asking me to join the elite group of ordinary people who all loved Josie. There was no junk in Josie's world - she collected top quality individuals in her life like other people collect salt and pepper shakers; she found them everywhere and kept them close. It was her enthusiasm people loved and were attracted to. And I ... I am deeply honored to have received this "by-invitation-only" and wouldn't miss Josie's life celebration event ... for anything in the world.

Nick

I spent weeks preparing the material for a presentation for a group of nineteen-year-olds. The banquet hall was full of noise and food. The message; "be your authentic self" and "pursue your heart's desire' and the money will follow". These 30 minutes were designed to inspire, convince, and encourage. The presentation was well received and I left the building that day with a sense of exhilaration and a natural high that comes with accomplishment.

The following weekend, with my presentation having been completed and behind me, I was going to take some time to relax.

Joe and I were joining friends on an eighty-passenger double-decker boat touring the mansion-laden shores of Lake Minnetonka. I had never been on the lake. As Joe and I stepped onto the double-decker boat I was ready to be 'wowed'.

The boat was being sold and the seller didn't feel obligated to leave the bar fully stocked for its upcoming new owners, thus today is designated for friends... and friends-of-friends to take the final cruise and clean out the bar. First of all, there was enough booze on the boat to facilitate a massive New Year's celebration in Time Square and second of all; by the looks of the guests on board...they had invited the wrong group to handle the assigned task.

The parade of expensive homes didn't hold my attention as much as the diversity of people that wandered the deck that day. The boat was packed, but there was one person in particular that peaked my curiosity. He was a 'leftover hippie' looking gentleman with hair longer than mine!! He was talking intensely with a young man. I didn't want to interrupt, but at the same time, I really wanted to meet them.

Later, I wandered to the back of the ship and said with a smile, "Hi, I'm Cathy; I'm always intimidated by guys who have hair longer than mine!" He chuckled and introduced himself. Then he took a step back and said, "I'd like you to meet my son, Nick". Nick took my offered hand and looked down at me from his towering frame.

Shaking his hand, I asked how old he was. "Nineteen" he replied still holding my gaze.

"Well, what are you doing now that you're out of high school?' I continued.

His height seemed to diminish as his eyes lowered to the floor. He said, "Well, uh, I was going to school at a junior college but I just recently quit". Then I understood the downcast eyes – the shame – he had confessed the mortal sin. After all, everyone knows it's a disgrace to opt out of college and the American Dream.

Stumbling over his words he said, "I'd really like to umm...well umm …work with sound on movies and umm... I was sort of – umm ...maybe – was thinking about going to California."

I listened as he spoke quietly and tentatively about his hopes and dreams. I joined him staring at the deck, both of us looking at the floor, as he voiced his doubts and fears and turmoil that had undoubtedly consumed their cruise conversation on the water that day.

Like a poker player with a Royal Flush in hand, I listened and waited.

When it was my turn, I pulled out a condensed version of all of the statistics, authoritative studies and powerful quotes that the past weeks of research had left at my fingertips. All the while, as I talked, his eyes were darting around, and his ears were cocked like a dog in a listening stance.

Slowly, point by point, I followed the outline in my head... ending the closing argument with;

> A twenty year study of 1500 people; tracked through the years of their professional lives. They were asked at the beginning to choose which group they would be in:

> Group # 1) to do what they **loved to do** regardless of the money

> OR

Group #2) work for **money now** during your career and do what you **love to do later** in life or after you retire.

The study ended with 101 participants becoming millionaires. Of the 101 millionaires ... 100 were from the group who did what they <u>loved to do</u>.

Nick and I locked eyes as the cruise ended and we pulled up next to the dock. The quiet exterior of this nineteen-year-old looked as if it was about to explode.

He stepped off the boat at full height with head up, shoulders back ... and I knew ... I *knew without one single doubt* that the weeks of research and preparation had *nothing* at all to do with a conference and *everything* to do with this <u>one</u> young man today.

As we stepped off the boat Nick's father came to shake my hand. Joe and I walked away together arm in arm and Joe's question was: "What was *that* all about?" All I could do was smile.

Life is a puzzle and sometimes we hold a piece that fits in someone else's life ... sometimes that piece is called inspiration ... sometimes it's called encouragement ... sometimes it's called approval . We all carry pieces that fit in another's life and that day I had a piece that fit in Nick's life.

... and once in a while I remember Nick ... like today ... when I opened this document ...

... or when I watch the credits roll at the end of a film ... or see the camera pan in or out ... and I *never* wonder if he is a 'success'... or if his name is famous ...

I actually wonder about myself ... I know that sounds strange ... but I wonder if I could sleep at night ... had I not stopped to talk to the Nick that day.

I know countless times I am in a particular place, at a particular time, for a particular reason that is NOT coincidence ... I am there to point someone in the direction of their BEST SELF ... and so I talk to people literally everywhere I go ... so that each night as I lay my head on the pillow ... I can sleep deeply...

Caramel Corn

John had just been home from college for the weekend, but somehow we really hadn't spent much time together.

Wanting him to know I was thinking of him, I did what any good mom would do, I got out the caramel corn recipe! This treat never fails to get AA++ rating whenever I make it. The response is *so* consistent, that I have started taking a copy of the recipe along with me whenever I am taking the treat to someone. It always happens that after they taste it they MUST have the recipe.

So I made three batches of this addicting concoction and packaged it in four large plastic bags, putting a name on each bag; one bag for each of John's college roommates. I packed all four bags in a big box and took it to the post office.

Several days later the box arrived at NDSU. As he was opening it John was joking with his friends. "What could I have possibly forgotten that was so important my mom shipped it to me?"

After he opened the box it revealed not just something for John – but, a 'mom gift' for all of them!!! My phone rang. I could hardly hear my son because in the background there were 3 college age young men SCREAMING and HOOTING their elation!!

I am sure the shipping on that box cost more than the contents of the package, but it was the best money I ever spent just to hear the four of them surprised and delighted, ready to devour the contents.

For readers who have never tasted this sweet sensation: You will find it is guaranteed to delight college age guys!

Best Ever Caramel Corn

6-8 quarts popped corn (3 bags Orville Redenbacher Smart Pop)

Mix 1 cup butter
1 1/2 cups sugar
1/2 cup white corn syrup
Bring to a boil and stir constantly (or use a Teflon pan - not so much stirring)
while slowly boiling for 15 minutes. Remove from heat and add 1 teaspoon vanilla. Pour over corn in a large buttered bowl. Pour onto waxed paper and cool.

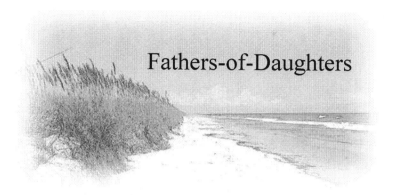

Fathers-of-Daughters

If I close my eyes I can see the whole series of events unfold.

I can just see those big eyes of my granddaughter and that cute little nose of hers and that thick blond hair as she chats with me over the phone about her doubts of starting middle school ... a new building ... lockers with combinations ... Is she going to be able to switch books quickly enough to get to the next class? And what about following the dress code? Will everything be okay making this change to a bigger school with older kids? All of these important questions to be answered.

And my son, the father of my granddaughter, is a wonderful dad and takes all of these things seriously.

Most recently, his daughter's iPhone5 charger is not working. It charges her phone to 29% and will not go beyond. So she asks her dad if he will get her a new charger. He assures his blond haired beauty that he will get her a charger.

"It needs to be a green charger!" she says emphatically, "It needs to be green!"

The following morning my son enters the Verizon store with the simple task of buying a green charger. He finds many different colors of chargers and none of them are green.

Knowing that this is important to his daughter, he chooses three from the rack. Not one, not two, but three different colors! One of the chargers' happens to be pink and purple, and he thinks that maybe this one will be adequate ... maybe, it will suffice instead of a green charger. So he purchases the three different chargers and leaves the Verizon store to get on with business for the rest of his day.

Arriving at a meeting with a businessman later that day, the businessman says, "Hang on a second, before we start, I have to charge my phone. " As the tumblers of the Universe all click into place, the man reaches in his briefcase and pulls out a green charger for his iPhone5 and plugs it in.

My son looks at him as if a miracle from the heavens has just descended upon him and asks casually, "Can I have that charger?" With a quizzical expression, the gentleman says "sure".

John said "No, I mean can I keep it?"

As John explains his beautiful daughter wants a green charger for her iPhone5 the other man smiles and conspiratorially looks at him and says, " I have three daughters of my own." The two 'fathers-of-daughters' passed an 'understanding' look between them ... a comradery with comments and smiles and laughs as John offered him his choice of the <u>three</u> new chargers from Verizon. The businessman chose the pink and purple one.

I don't know what kind of work-related discussion the two men conducted that day. I don't know if it was about machines or manufacturing or something as monumental as an international peace treaty...but I do know that John left with the prize ... the really BIG prize ... to go home that night and deliver to his daughter exactly what he had promised.

I don't know if he ever told his daughter where the charger came from...and it doesn't matter. What I know for sure is ... one father came to the aid of another father ... letting my son go home that night ... as a hero ... for his daughter ... his beautiful adorable daughter ... the most important client he will *ever* have.

Brady's Life Lesson
September 9-2005

Phoenix Arizona (Brady 8 years old)

"Brady had a life lesson today" my son said as we talked on the phone. "Tell me more" I said as I instinctively grabbed a pen and paper to take notes at the same time.

My son and his son stopped at the grocery store today, Friday afternoon after work/school and were on their way to pick up some Light beer and hard salami for the weekend.

My son continues, "Driving the company truck with a topper makes it hard to have clear vision backing out of a parking spot, so we parked at the back of the lot pulling forward into an empty stall, and then I don't have to back up the truck."

He said "Getting out of the vehicle, there was a man sitting on the turned down tail gate of his truck next to us. As we headed toward the store the man asked if I had any cash I could give him, as he was out of gas. I told him, "I never carry cash. Sorry about that." ... and the man on the tailgate said "No problem, I'll find someone to give me a hand."

"So Brady and I went shopping and at the check-out counter, besides paying for the groceries I got $10 cash from my debit card."

"Brady wanted to know why I had gotten cash back and if the money was for him. :-) This was a new situation. All he had ever seen was simply paying with a card, never getting cash back." John explained to him, "I got the money for the man outside."

Excitedly Brady said, 'Well dad, maybe he won't be there anymore when we get back out there!' I chuckled and agreed; maybe he won't be there anymore." Then Brady asked me "If the guy isn't there can I have the money?" and laughing I said "Well, we'll see."

"In the parking lot as we approached our vehicle, the man was still there and was getting a couple of dollars from another shopper about to enter the store."

"I walked up to him and said "Here, this is for you" and handed him $10. The guy said "Hey thanks! Thanks a lot!" and proceeded to hand back $2 to the previous shopper saying, "Here you take this back, I don't need it now."

"When Brady and I got in the vehicle to go home I asked Brady 'Why did we give money to that man?' Brady said "I don't know."

"I said 'because someday you might need some help – and wouldn't you like it if somebody helped you?' and Brady agreed he would."

John was teaching his son a lesson certainly … about compassion and giving and all that this includes.

And yet, at the same time, as a parent I know it was more.

It was about insurance … when you believe 'what goes around comes around' ... when you believe 'what goes *out* is what comes *back*' ....when you believe what you sew is what you reap – then, as a parent, it IS insurance ... or a *profound prayer* ... *a prayer* for the day ... that *your* son or *your* daughter is in need ... a hope that a stranger like *you* ... will step forward and say ... "Here this is for you."

The Baton Man

There's a man who takes a walk every morning along the shoulder of the highway I drive to town on each day. He wears a reflective vest and carries a baton in his hand along with a ready wave and a smile for every car that goes by.

The first time I saw the man waving to every car I was taken by surprise. I just smiled to myself and gave a little wave back.

On following days, when I would see the man on the side of the road walking, I would begin early and raise my hand to wave.

As time has gone by, I made my wave BIGGER and put an even BIGGER smile on my face. Now, my wave is large and my smile is huge because I not only *want* to smile, but I want to *encourage* him! Not only is he keeping his body physically fit but he's filling that place inside himself, that connects him with the rest of humanity ... not just the part of humanity he personally knows, but us all!

I don't know the man; I've never met him face to face, voice to voice, or heart to heart. And yet, I am quite sure that he has done this his entire life. Not in the same way perhaps ...

147

not with a baton in his hand walking along the road ... but with words and gestures of kindness.

Let's face it, someone who never connects with people in regular everyday life, would not make themselves a target of teasing, by walking along the road with a baton in hand. This guy is *animated* about celebrating life and I am betting he takes every opportunity to make *life* better for others in every way he can ... someday I will have to stop and meet him.

Coincidence

I had the most perfect summer job imaginable! A lovely couple, who wanted thousands of blooming flowers in their yard and on their patio, hired me to plant and tend these growing jewels all summer. Whenever the time fit for me, I could plant and play in the dirt. Often times I was at their lake home at 7 AM with the water sparkling and not a soul around except for the morning bees feasting on the roses. Sometimes I was there so early I had to dodge the water sprinklers that were methodically cascading across the yard.

The flowers were all chosen in the colors that matched the inside decor of the home. I had read once that Barbara Streisand chose her flower colors this way as well. So, often as I deadheaded flowers, I would find the melody of ♫You Don't Bring Me Flowers Anymore ♫ floating through my mind as I worked.

It wasn't until I was inside their house one day and looked out at the flowers, I realized what a breathtaking effect it had. It was as if the home itself had invited the flowers and patio inside as a guest.

Each spring even with the back seats folded down in my van and the passenger seat loaded with flowers, it still took two trips to the greenhouse to collect all the plants needed for this project.

For eight years I have relied on one man and his greenhouses to supply me with 1200 to 1400 flowers each spring. Now I had to face the fact that Chippewa Farms Nursery was no longer in business. I had to write up an order to another establishment. I would miss Marc. He was always pleasant, conversational, and interested in my planting project. He was always efficient and prepared with my order at planting time. I will miss the man.

And so this past Monday was my first day with a new guy. One of our local grocery stores does ordering of semi-loads of flowers each year. The new guy said he'd be happy to take my order. I finally had the order ready in hand, on Monday. However, at about 11:30 AM that morning the new guy was gone and I was asked to come back later if I could. "No problem" I told a gal behind the checkout counter, "I'll be back".

45 minutes later I returned to the store.

I spent a couple minutes explaining to the new guy what I needed. Then leaving the store, walking across the parking lot...I saw Marc! "Marc!" I said "This it too strange! I was here turning in my order for flowers and HERE YOU ARE!"

We chatted for a bit about planting season and then he said to me quietly, "Nine years ago today my wife died and my son called and asked me to pick up flowers for her grave." He smiled gently and said " It's kind of ironic isn't it ... me

... buying flowers?" I agreed as his mind wandered away to thoughts of his wife, I suspect.

I stood there taking in the information...the man who had planted and grown flowers by the gazillions was here...buying flowers for his wife. Again Barbara Streisand was in my head singing, ♫'You Don't Bring Me Flowers Anymore'. ♫

I don't believe in coincidence. There are too many times that happenstance just isn't coincidence. I think I was there to *hear* Marc talk ... so he could tell someone else, that even though this time he didn't grow them himself, he was taking flowers to the woman of his dreams ... there are all kinds of tragic ends to love stories, yet somehow ... I doubt ... Marc's wife will *ever* be singing ♫You Don't Bring Me Flowers Anymore♫.

At the Library

Two boys were standing at one of the library check out stations, as I stood at the other window waiting, as a librarian retrieved a reserved item I had been waiting for.

The two boys, just a few feet away, though about the same height, were opposite skin colors. The one was white blond, beyond pale actually, and the other black, beyond brown. There they stood side by side as the librarian put the scanner to their library card. The computer beeped. She told them there were $2.00 worth of fines and asked if they had any money with them. They glanced guiltily sideways at each other with a bit of fear creeping in. Looking back at the librarian they both silently shook their heads 'NO'. The librarian was about to bypass the fee in the computer and said they could pay it next time they came in.

I interjected, "I'll pay that!"

Relief washed over their faces as I handed over the money. Now, they didn't have to go home and tell anyone there was a fine waiting to be paid.

The young boys said nothing and checked out their books. When I was finished at the desk, I stepped out into the sunshine to find the two young boys holding their bikes. They had waited for me and thanked me profusely for paying the fine and then road away, side by side, black and white, ebony and ivory.

I always volunteer to pay fines for people at the library. It's not just a kindness on my part. It is a deep belief that ANYTHING we want to learn can be found in books ... and this service that is free to all, creates a level playing field between those who have money and those who do not.

For many it is a place of calm ... a place to find age-old wisdom ... a place to find an archive of learning and understanding that touches every single area of interest known to mankind.

I have personally talked to people who have driven forty miles to take advantage of a free pancake breakfast ... while at the same time, behind the doors of a library ... is a free *smorgasbord* ... of **thoughts** and **ideas** at no cost ... big helpings of **art** and **science** ... a full platter of the rich **history** of the world ... the universe ...the solar system ... **philosophy** and politics ... sewing and gardening ... fiction and non-fiction.

I want those two young boys to know their library card is infinitely more powerful than a credit card ... their library card offers to all ... the riches ... we call ... **knowledge**.

Twindom

A beauty shop is a most interesting place.

He wasn't talking to me, I was just listening. As he was getting his hair cut, the man in the chair said he had a set of twin boys as well as a daughter. He and his wife had had many miscarriages and decided to apply for adoption. When the agency finally called, the couple was asked if they would take a set of TWINS! The adoption agency wanted to keep the babies together if at all possible…

I exclaimed, "You lucky duck!"

Growing up as a twin myself, I know how fortunate these two boys are. They have a built-in lifelong best friend. Someone to call and ask, "Do you remember this event happening this way when we were seven?"

When you're a twin you never assume you are alone. The only feeling I can equate the twin-bond with is the love between a child and a parent...a profound bottomless love that develops minute by minute throughout a lifetime. It doesn't come from DNA; it comes from the progression of time and moments together.

I read about two couples in another country who ended up getting the wrong babies during their stay in a maternity hospital ward. The error was discovered seven years later. When the parents were informed that they had each gotten the wrong baby, both sets of parents agreed ... they wanted to keep the child they had been raising for years. Step by step ... moment by moment... one heartbeat after another ... love grows.

All my steps have been side by side with Carol ... walking the earth ... knowing that she is the one human being alive that I have shared the entire progression of this lifetime ...

◆◆◆◆◆◆◆◆◆

To My Twin Sister

If I die before you ...

Will you sit with my sons when they long to have me back?

Will you talk to them when they need to ask questions they wish they had asked when I was here?

Will you calm their regrets – for surely there will be some – no life lived is ever complete without regrets. ☺

Will you be their 'Aunt Eileen'? The one who will tell them stories of their mother's childhood with truth and humor?

Will you chaperone my grandchildren through holidays and graduations and deaths as best you can?

Will you talk to me through the layers of clouds and gods?

When it is your time to cross over will you remember that I will be the FIRST one waiting for you on the other side and you will not fear?

And if, God forbid, you should be the first of us to leave, I will do, to the best of my ability, all of the above for your son, granddaughter and any other loved ones who join your family in the years ahead.

I treasure the joint life we share. It's an unseen shield that protects the two of us together that the rest of the world neither knows nor sees. I pity others for this...I really do!

And so, my lifelong friend and companion, I close with words that sound trite compared to my depth of feeling.

I love you,

Cathy

◆◆◆◆◆◆◆◆◆◆

A Toast to Sisters

She was working behind the teller's window at the bank that day, just making small talk with me as I handed over the checks to be cashed. The name plate on the wall said Brenda. Most of the people at the teller line I knew by name, but not Brenda ... not yet anyway.

I immediately noticed Brenda's Dress and I said "I love your dress! "

"Really!?!" she smiled brightly

"Yes, I love the pin tucks on the top!"

"Thank you!" she said casually, "My sister bought me this dress! " She said brightly!

"How great is THAT!" I said.

"Yes", she said (big sigh) "but she died!" Not even stopping to pause or take a breath she rattled on "…but we did everything together until the end … I would climb into her hospital bed (now her enthusiasm increasing) and we shopped together (even more excitement in her voice and face) … on the internet … and she bought me this dress…and we ate ice cream together! And not one of her nurses ever complained about it … well …except one nurse! That nurse complained when we started eating our *second* Dairy Queen Blizzard together."

Without pausing for breath she sighed and said   "I miss her!" She sighed again … as if remembering the absent sister. She took a breath and simply looked at me waiting to join her celebration of life, so I said "I'm going to Owatonna this weekend !!! And meeting my twin sister at a hotel…" I blurted out! " …she's driving three hours and I'm driving three hours and we are meeting in the middle…it's a rendezvous of sorts and time to talk with no interruptions ... just the two of us!. "

The tellers eyes lit up! "What fun!" she said and I knew the picture in her mind was of she and her sister together. "While you're there" she said excitedly "make a toast to me and my sister!!"

157

"We will!" I said enthusiastically. "I already have the wine and wine glasses packed!" I retorted

Before leaving the bank that morning I said "Brenda – you made my day – thank you!"

So, my twin and I lounged in our hotel room talking the day and night away. We opened a bottle of wine and as I put the two-piece plastic wine glasses together...before our first sip I said to my twin sister "Wait!... wait!... wait! I have to tell you a story first."

I told her about Brenda at the bank that morning as Carol and I sat in a hotel room with our glasses of wine ... toasting two other sisters who did it right ... laughing ... and loving ... and shopping ... and eating Dairy Queen to the very end.

Target Field

It was a magic moment as Joe and I entered Target Field for my *very first* professional baseball game…there was high energy coming from all 31,457 people. Two country bumpkins; Joe and I were thinking we would have to use GPS to determine our walking route from the hotel to Target field…dah! We just followed the flow of TWINS shirts…go figure!

Seriously … there's a long line of people waiting to take their selfies sitting inside the massive baseball glove sculpture! Really?" We're from the country, we don't DO LINES! So we strolled and gawked, trying to blend, but it was useless, we were the Beverly Hillbillies arriving in the city…and we didn't give a hoot.

Wide eyed, I asked the dumbest questions and nobody seemed to mind. Inside the stadium, delightful attendants kept moving us along closer and closer to the seats that were gifted to us…lower and lower…and lower and lower we went until we came to an attendant who had to see our tickets before we could pass through the lower gate…OMG! Eleven rows from the field! The Twins mascot was up close and personal ... <u>all of it was</u>! This was royalty seating!!!!

A family arrived in front of us with three little boys, all carrying baseball gloves. They assured me that if a ball came our way, *they* would handle the situation. I didn't bring a glove – I had been thinking about bringing binoculars ... clearly, I needed none.

Shortly before game time, a young intelligent looking man with glasses and pale white skin sat next to me. Behind him followed a tall large mature comfortably dressed black man. As the game commenced, the two carried on a conversation in my right ear ... their conversation becoming a part of my experience.

The young man is a recent college graduate and wants to be a public speaker. He is thinking about it seriously. The older/wiser black man is telling him he needs to take his risks now, before he has responsibilities ... now is the time to give it your ALL if you want to own a business ... now is the time you can sleep on a sofa.

The older/wiser man continues to weave a story of depriving himself as he built his own business, telling the younger man that he too can do this. The older/wiser gentleman has been to other countries and knows that *here*, in America, is the land of opportunity. The two are in Toastmasters together and continue to discuss public speaking as a viable business.

At the same time they are watching me ... as I jump up and cheer. They stare as I joyously take part in "the wave' which I have only seen on TV until this very moment. I am listening to them and yet I am not. There is so much to see and hear.

Finally older/wiser black man is saying that he is currently taking a Dale Carnegie course … and suggests that the young man do the same.

At this point unable to stay out of the conversation one second longer I reached across the young man, pointing at the arm of the older/wiser black man. To the young man I asked, "What does this man do, that makes him a riveting speaker?" The black man looks at me and says "**I'm** a riveting speaker?"

Now I spoke directly to him. "Yes, yes you are…you are a riveting speaker because you can tell a story and teach at the same time." Now, touching the black man's arm I looked right into the eyes of the young white man and said, "Everything that this man has told you is *absolutely* true … you *need* to listen to him."

With lightning speed I returned my attention to the game. The two of them looked stunned that I easily and efficiently simply entered their conversation and then turned around and left their discussion … back to the game as childish delight came bubbling out again … oh goody, it was time for another WAVE!!!

This game had EVERYTHING! Constant entertainment – I had no idea, when the television cameras cut to a commercial between innings, that there is always entertainment on the baseball field …who knew? I had no idea that the cameras were on people in the audience … a young boy about 10 years old was captured dancing on the steps near us.

Food … beer … bright lights … entertainment … 4th of July fireworks … an intelligent thought provoking conversation going on next to me … it was all a magical mix ... indeed there is opportunity ... and *truly* there is hope ... when a caring wise older man mentors a young intellectual man ... on the first base line ... at Target Field.

Rochester, Minnesota

Back in 2005 my mom and dad were visiting the Mayo Clinic for routine every-other-year complete physicals and checkups. I know, not many people have the luxury of living within driving distance of such a renowned medical facility, but they did and they took advantage of it.

People from all over the world come to Rochester, MN. Dad told me that one time while they were there; there was a King in the facility.

Years later I was listening to an audio book by Queen Noir, Queen of Jordan and the widow of the late King Hussein. As I listened to her tell her story she began to talk about her and her husband's trips to the Mayo Clinic in Rochester Minnesota and I knew that *this* was what dad had been talking about.

One night Joe and I booked a room at the same hotel that Mom and Dad were staying at, to spend a night there, helping them to pass a quiet evening in Rochester. We knew that the days drug on for them, with no one there that they knew. So we shared an evening just passing time and visiting.

Joe and I got up early the next morning to leave for home while Mom and Dad would be checking out later that day.

I went to the front desk to pay our bill and then asked the man behind the counter if my dad had paid for their weeks' stay yet. He said "no" and I told him I wanted to pay the bill. I asked for a piece of notepaper and simply wrote across it...

"Dad, you've done so much for me…how can I ever repay you? Your room is my gift. I love you, Cathy" and handed it back to the man and asked him to give it to my dad when he came to check out.

Later that week I talked to dad on the phone and he said the man at the hotel said "What a daughter!" and dad assured me that he treasured the gift and the values I choose to live by.

Now when I think back, it makes me smile, almost makes me laugh actually, because HE was the one who taught me how to give…

◆◆◆◆◆◆◆◆◆◆

This coming month I get to go to Phoenix. I will get to spend six days taking care of my precious 12 year old granddaughter while her parents are gone on vacation. We will be free to do whatever we want!

After I arranged for the flight my son said, "Hey Mom, when you get that confirmation email, shoot it over to me so I can put your flight times in my calendar".

Sure, no problem.

A few days later I opened my office door and a piece of mail had been pushed under the door. That was rather strange…it must have been delivered to the wrong box in the bank of mailboxes outside the building and someone brought it to my door and slid it under.

I saw that the envelope was from Phoenix and it was in my son's handwriting. Not having a clue why he would send something in the mail, I opened the envelope. A card said THANK YOU on the front and inside a note from my son saying...

"Hey Mom, Thanks so much for coming to stay with Maggie next month. I'm sure you two are going to have a great time! Love you! John"

Enclosed was a check for my airfare.

◆◆◆◆◆◆◆◆◆

I wonder if my dad had any idea that his sense of kindness has already passed to **two** generations; first through me and then on to my children. I remember one time, when I was in college, dad saying to me, "You know ... only one generation will remember you."

Then in my late teens, a thought that deep had never EVER entered my mind! I was concerned with grades at college and the fit of my bell-bottom jeans for crying out loud!

If my dad were to say to me now, "You know, only one generation will remember you." I would say to him "I'm good with that."

Carrying on my legacy for more generations than this one has no interest to me. I drive by named buildings every day, and I wonder who that person might have been. My granddaughter's middle school in Phoenix is named after someone. Parks and roadways and street names are all trying to keep a legacy alive beyond one lifetime, and I have no idea who they were and I know my dad was right about this.

But one thing my dad didn't think about, was that there are inheritances more noteworthy than a name ... there are birthrights more important than money ... and there are endowments more significant than family heirlooms.

So, Dad was right, his name will not go on the side of a building or street sign or a community park. There will be no airport or stadium named after him. What will follow his lifetime is the *significance of his principles* ... his willingness to *give to others* ... his *kind-heartedness* will carry on from generation to generation ... a legacy more *meaningful* ... than he ever could have imagined.

Priceless
6-14-2005

Today I am sorting an entire lifetime of stuff and among the articles I found this morning was a pair of shoes; teeny tiny toddler shoes. Robbie's shoes - so small they did not fill the flat of my open hand. The toes were worn completely down to the fabric from crawling on the floor. I always loved those shoes on him, tan in color and a high top style with matching shoelaces.

As I sorted, I knew that Rob would soon be leaving for Denver for four months to work and he would be on his own, knowing almost no one there.

Looking at the tiny small shoes I sat at the table with pen in hand and wrote – *the child that wore these shoes is more precious to me than the world. I always thought he would be small and near my legs...never leaving my side – and now he will be going to Denver, Please take careful steps and keep my child safe – to soon return to my arms.*

I cried over the box as I put the shoes all by themselves inside and addressed it to Robbie.

I took the box to our small town post office and carefully handed the precious cargo over to the man behind the counter..."Need any insurance or confirmation of delivery? Anything fragile, breakable or hazardous?" he asked as his repetitive voice trailed off.

I thought to myself; you have no idea what is *really* in this box. There is no insurance in the world that could replace these. These shoes were on my son's feet when he went from crawling to walking. They were a protection for his first steps...they watched the direction of his life as it began...and created balance for him to stand on. His first steps created the beliefs that direct every stride of his life now...this is where his foundation began.

There are outrageous insurance policies for irreplaceable objects and pieces of art ... but I know what priceless is ... priceless ... was in that box.

The Power Washer

I had never used a power washer on anything in my life, until the day that the boulders arrived.

I asked for a pile of rocks in the yard. I was asking for just a discreet pile to be hauled into the yard from around our fields. The picture I had in my mind was a small arrangement about 8 feet wide. What I got was quite different! It ended up being a full day of work with a large dump trailer, a tractor and a mini excavator depositing 40 feet of boulders. I got to ride on the excavator and direct the exact positioning of the rocks. Joe and our friend Mark were boys playing with very BIG toys! All I had to do was feed them for the day and they were happy to work like dogs!

All the boulders had been lying around the outside edges of the farm fields for decades and all of them were covered with moss and scale and dirt so that the massive pile of stones all looked the same.

Of course they needed to be washed and it was suggested that _someone_ should power wash the stones.

So on a sunny day, I asked Joe to set up the power washer for me and give me a quick lesson in how to use this piece of equipment. It looked _easy_; I had _watched_ it in use many times.

I was prepared; wearing galoshes and ear protection and sunglasses to shield my eyes. And yet the first time I pulled the trigger on the wand, the sheer pressure pushed me backward several steps, and I caught my balance shooting water high up into the air. I was shocked at the force behind it.

Now I held on tight to the wand. At first I stood back from the stones as I washed, thinking that I could somehow stay clean. Boy was I wrong! I had no idea how close I would have to be to the rocks in order for the water to peel off the decades of scale and slime that had accumulated. Neither did I have any idea how much water and dirt would be _coming back at me_ during the process. At first I fought against the water wanting to stay back and not get wet and dirty. Finally I realized that it was inevitably a part of the process, then I let go ... and enjoyed it.

I began slowly and methodically uncovering the beauty underneath all of that dirt and the scale and the slime ...one by one the real beauty of each stone appeared. At times I was shocked to find a white rock or a rock that had lines running through it or a boulder with pink tones and black speckles.

I got more and more excited each time I started cleaning another boulder ... knowing that under each one was a great surprise. Some had holes and crevices that made you wish they could tell you their story. Others had cracks that you would swear it would simply fall into two pieces, or you could just put your fingers inside and pull the stone layers apart and yet it stayed together.

Two ginormous rocks that both looked like half of a hard-boiled egg cut horizontally, looked as if you put the two halves together, it would make a whole egg again, and I can't know if that was true.

I found myself trying to imagine the history behind each rock. And I wonder if it felt good to be clean and to let the beauty out. I wonder if it felt good to have someone there admiring and revealing the hard strength that had been hidden inside for so long. I wonder if it felt good to have someone digging through the tall grass searching for you… finally, looking for your unique beauty and your history, and doing all of that for no reason other than the pure beauty of it. These rocks that were once forgotten for decades were now chosen by two people to be the backdrop of a garden. Now the rain will fall gently on them and there will be flowers blooming and ferns growing among these rocks.

The wind carried the dirt and grime that day, to my freshly washed windows on the house ... and I didn't care at all ... I was filthy with water inside my boots … my clothes were wet and stuck to my skin … my hair was heavy with grit ... and I never felt better in my life!

Fire Breathing Dragon

She was brutally honest with her words. As I heard them the fires of anger were being thrown from my nostrils like a fire breathing dragon.

I'll show her I thought.

Here I was… pregnant for the third time and what a rude and cruel comment for someone to make. She said "If you don't get them two boys under control, you are going to have big problems when the third one comes along."

I mean after all I thought … here I was taking two toddlers with me, pregnant besides, as well as working a full work week. How was I supposed to do it all? How to discipline and have well behaved children? And why did I feel such anger inside me? Gradually I realized the anger was because, I knew it was TRUE! My two young sons were out of control.

The next day she arrived at my door holding a vase with three pink carnations and an apology on the tip of her tongue. Her husband had noticed my anger the day before and asked what in the world she had said to upset me…and here she was to apologize.

Where had I gone wrong? The answer was, I had gone wrong just one little step at a time just letting things go, when I was too tired to deal with the constant reminders and reinforcement they needed as toddlers.

Well, <u>that</u> day changed our lives.

I began…

I explained to the two boys that I had let them get out of hand, that it was *my* fault and that I was changing *my* ways. Every behavior that was unacceptable became a new mission for me. It took three weeks of sticking to my word, when they realized that I really meant what I had said. The behavior bar was raised to a higher rung and soon we all were enjoying life.

A decade later…

One day I was interviewing with a prospective mother for two openings in my daycare. My sons knew they were not to interrupt an interview. But John evidentially needed the answer to a question immediately. He entered the conversation by respectfully saying, "Excuse me Mom."

I introduced him to the woman sitting across the table – he shook her hand and said he was very pleased to meet her. John asked his question and turned to leave the room. At the front door he turned to the woman and said, "It was very nice to have met you."

I returned to the papers on the table but she stopped the interview.

"Never mind with the interview," she said "I want my children in *this* daycare … because I want my children to behave *that way* when they're grown up."

By this time, it was nothing out of the ordinary … it was respect … it was courtesy … it was politeness. I expected nothing less.

And my mind goes back to a day when the boys were toddlers ... to the day when a friend said exactly what I needed to hear … the day when a friend made me mad … the day when a friend made me look at myself. I have told this friend many times, how much I appreciate the anger she created in me ... and I am forever grateful.

John's 16th Birthday

John was playing in a Friday night, high school basketball game on the evening of his 16th birthday, so I called the school and asked the coach if I could buy pizza for the team after the game in celebration.

When John got home after the game he said the team was all thrilled that John had a birthday and they got to share the pizza!

John said, "Before the game started, we were all in the huddle and the coach said 'We don't lose at home! And we don't lose on John's birthday!"

... and they didn't.

Murray

My husband, Joe has always owned BIG dogs; the kind that would never be allowed in bed.

When our son Tom got his **first** Yorkie, Mason, if Joe and I were 'doggie-sitting' it was *out of the question that the dog would sleep with us.* Of course I respect Joe's view, *when Joe is at home.* And when Joe was NOT at home I reserve the right to make my own decision ... thank you very much!

How Tom received Murray his **second** Yorkie is a tale worth telling.

One fateful below zero temperature day, Tom saw a Yorkie on the street near his home in Fergus Falls. The little dog was lost and freezing, trying to lift his paws off the frozen ground with no owner in sight.

The little dog was an invalid of sorts; a Yorkie in pretty tough shape. Tom brought him inside, warmed him up, gave him food and water and then took him to the vet. The veterinarian put him on antibiotics and said that most of his teeth needed to be removed – they were rotten from never eating hard food that cleans the surface of the teeth …his fur wreaked of cigarette smoke and his ribs were visible under the mangy fur.

As the dog slowly began recovering Tom wanted to permanently keep the little fellow, but knowing how much he would miss his own dog were he ever to get lost, Tom decided to put a 'lost dog' ad in the newspaper, hoping that no one would respond.

A local couple called and said they had lost the dog. With misgivings Tom returned the little dog to its owners. The two people were at home, watching TV and smoking cigarettes on the afternoon he delivered the dog back to its home. It was hard to 'do the right thing' in this situation because Tom knew that the little guy wasn't being cared for properly.

Finally a friend of Tom's suggested that he call or write a letter to the owners and offer to buy the dog. Since he knew where the people lived, Tom dropped off a handwritten note into their mail box offering to buy the dog.

45 minutes after the note was delivered Tom's phone rang. The person on the phone said, "Ya, you said you might be interested in buying this dog? How much would you be willing to pay?"

Tom said, "Well, I've spent about $100 to $125 on vet bills already, I suppose I'd be willing to pay $50 to $100."

Without hesitation the owner replied "You come up with 100 bucks and the dog is *yours!*"

As Tom returned to the smoke filled home with $100 in hand, the little Yorkie was jumping and running around Tom, ready to go! And *that* is how Tom got a second Yorkie now named Murray…with 15 teeth removed just a week ago … healthfully plump … no visible ribs now … watched and cared for every day.

And we think how lucky for the dog – when in reality – how lucky for *all* of us – now Murray has become a part of our family too.

◆◆◆◆◆◆◆◆◆◆

Joe is gone on a fishing trip this weekend. It's a lazy Sunday morning and I am almost alone in my bed. On my left side is Murray and on my right is Mason. I look down to see if they are awake and two sets of eyes look back at me.

Lazy ... lazy ... all three of us together. Then Murray begins to weasel his way up to my neck. A minute later Mason inches his way into my neck on the other side.

I have two arms wrapped around dogs – in bed - Sunday morning ... with soft warm breathing on my neck and all three of us are content to doze off again... :-)

Selling Land

It was an evening of memories for me, just driving the well-worn back roads to my mom and dad's house. They don't live there anymore but the road was the same. A group of local snowmobilers are thinking about buying a piece of the land that has been in our possession for seven years since Mom and Dad passed.

This sunny bright evening I got out of my vehicle to look at mom and dad's land – the low areas and high ground – the strip of evergreens that volunteered to grow decades ago. I felt warm on the outside and the inside.

With time to spare I drove through the town to see a new park and new businesses and I stopped at the church. It had the same Ironwork decorative stairs with open spaces – I walked slowly up the steps to the church letting the memories flood the empty space. The doors were locked ... a sign of the times. The church was always unlocked when I was a little girl.

I went to Plantenburg's grocery store where a hometown meat shop still operates. I decided that today I was going to buy meat and a bag of ice to lay on top of it – this negotiation probably wouldn't take long.

The whole time, the quiet in my mind was enjoying the past of my childhood. Handing over my credit card to the clerk I looked up to see my niece entering the store. I was thrilled that after all these years I would happen to meet someone I knew in my old hometown.

I arrived at the meeting right on time and found a group of people, all genuine and sharing who they are. One man was introduced as a former dentist and I gawked at him. Could it be my dentist from when I was small? No it's not possible! He seemed so old when I was little! He looked at me and asked if I have a twin sister? "Yes" I said. I guess that was that. He sure didn't look very old to me right now!

I was given a tour of the building they were hoping to replace and a verbal overview of their expectations for the future. The Snowcruiser Organization wanted a new location with a community building and room for parking and trail grooming equipment on our property if possible.

The president of the Snowmobile Club was trying to draw an approximate layout of the land on a dry marker board. I reached for the file of perfectly drawn maps I had brought with me and said "Do you know what my husband does for a living?"

One gentleman quipped "He's not an attorney is he?" I laughed and said "No, he's a surveyor and map-maker!"

The maps, precisely created by Joe, showed the property divided into detailed ½ acre sections all color coded and flawless. The discussion all of sudden became easy with the right tools. Joe always tells me, anything is easy with the right tools.

Looking at the land and talking, they were telling me what *they* wanted and when I interjected what would be good for *our family* the discussion immediately shifted to accommodate *both of us*.

I had walked into that meeting alone...with no fear whatsoever. There was no bantering, no bickering; nobody was trying to get more than their fair share. It was just a bunch of country folks, all of us, talking and honestly wanting for each other, to have, what the other wanted and needed.

In my bag I left with a signed agreement and so did they. I got exactly what *I* wanted and so did *they*. I walked away from that meeting having been filled up by the goodness of small town people ... loving it ... and its people ... now, even more than before.

Will 12 Students Return?

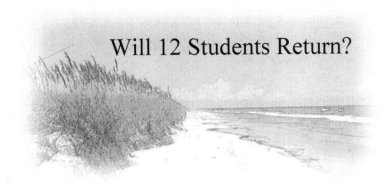

I entered the classroom curious to meet the other students who had chosen this course. My inner excitement was running high. This was my first time at the renowned summer writing program at the University of Iowa and I was serious. For weeks I researched the class offerings and professors as if my life depended on it. I ordered and read books by each author/professor I was considering...I had chosen well and so had the other eleven in the class.

"I've never had a group like this," said Stephen Bloom, journalism instructor. "Most summer classes are a social event and they follow an arch of interest. On Monday, the students are excited to learn, and by Friday they are ready to go home...but *not this class*! *Every* session ran late...you *never* stopped asking questions! You are relentless!" said Bloom, author of *Postville* and the upcoming *Tears of Mermaids*.

Yes, I was one of *those* 12 merciless students. We were all late arriving for Friday's *closing banquet* and Bloom, himself, had to give the banquet's concluding comments, so we *had* to leave the classroom, but we weren't done asking questions yet!

Across the banquet table, Bloom asked me, "Will you come back next summer?"

I countered his question with a question. "Will *you be teaching* next summer?"

"I'm exhausted!" he replied

"Of course you are," I said. "You have twelve intense students who all WANT to be here. Nobody is taking this class just to get credits for a degree. Nobody here cares about a grade point average. This is the ultimate learning situation, we are here by choice!"

I repeated my question. "Will you be teaching again next summer?"

Five minutes later he finally answered the inquiry. "The only way I would teach next summer is if *all 12 of you* came back for an advanced class".

Stunned, the 11 of us (one student had to leave a day early) passed glances around the banquet table with a question in everyone's eyes. We had come from all over the United States for this opportunity. Was it possible that travel plans, vacation time and commitment could bring the twelve of us back together next year to the green sunny campus in Iowa City, Iowa?

I didn't answer his question. We had a choice before us. Go home and USE what we had learned and come back next year OR take the easy way out and just go home. Ah hah! There was the crux of the matter, *if we come back next year, we will be held accountable,* either by ourselves or by classmates *to have actually USED what we learned.*

After completing his class my brain was screaming with information and possibilities. He had given us his most powerful tools for journalism and now the twelve of us had to decide *if* and *how to use it all.*

Each student had been offered time during our one-week course, to have a one-on-one writing consultation with the professor. When it was my turn, I quietly entered his private writing space and took in the details to see what the surroundings of a strong-minded writer would look like. My meeting with the professor was the very last day of class. I was not going to pass up the opportunity, to have someone of his caliber work with me.

He was at his computer looking absorbed as I entered. He looked surprised, as though he had forgotten a world outside of the one he was creating, actually existed.

"What do you want to write?" he asked

"Small monumental moments" I replied.

He leaned back in his chair and said, "Do it! That is totally what life is made of. There is material everywhere." My short time alone with him was intense ... encouraging ... and motivating.

Throughout the week of class we were asked to keep our professional occupation a secret from one another. It made the playing field level and someone else's degrees and accomplishments would intimidate no one. It also raised a question that is not often asked in our society, "Who am I without my job? Who am I *really?*"

So, late Friday afternoon, when we were *supposed to be* at the banquet hall, this was our time to discover what we all do professionally. The student that left a day early is a minister who had to perform a wedding ceremony. I do motivational speaking. As the profession game unfolded we found one to be a college teacher and yet another a high school journalism instructor. The professions were as varied as the writing projects that brought them to Iowa City.

Will the diverse and scattered class gather together next year in the halls of journalism? Will we all come back? Will any have accomplished the vast goals they shared with one another?

Will all twelve return next summer?…I don't know.

But I do know I was privileged to be a part of a group of 12 people that were there by choice for serious work. I know it was transformative for the twelve of us and perhaps for the professor as well.

This man has taught countless summer classes and it was gratifying to find out, on that final day, that we were the ones who challenged him and brought out the deep stuff. I think that perhaps it had been a long time since he had seen such hungry students. Maybe it refreshed his belief in being a teacher. I hope that when he's talking to other professors about students and learning he will say, "Let me tell you about a summer class I had one time..."

◆◆◆◆◆◆◆◆◆

Professor Bloom decided not to teach the following summer, opting to work on his own writing projects; being obsessed by them.

I wish I could tell you that I came right home from Iowa and 'got on' with writing this book. Instead I let it sit there while continually creating more and more files of small monumental moments that needed fleshing out.

As it grew bigger, it felt as if the folder itself was screaming at me to please write it! So here I am, doing just that. I think I waited these four years since being in Iowa because I knew ... I knew that once the folder was opened ... I too ... would be obsessed.

As the files multiplied and grew I recognized that Bloom was absolutely correct ... everywhere you go ... each experience in life ... is a constant flow of material ... even sitting right there in his classroom ... the twelve of us together.

In a matter of weeks this book will be complete ... then I will sign and send a copy ... of these small monumental moments ... along with my gratitude ... to a man who gave his BEST to twelve hungry students ... on the green and lush campus in Iowa City, Iowa.

Scraps of Paper

Without thinking …I reload the paper into the printer.
Without thinking… I reach for decorative notepads on my desktop.
Without thinking…I reach for the scratchpad next to my telephone.
Without thinking … I reach for the pen next to my reading chair.
Paper, pens, and mechanical pencils; everything at my fingertips.

My mom used to save old envelopes and discarded paper with blank space on the back. She would methodically cut them into small pieces and stack them in her 'junk drawer' for grocery lists and reminder notes.

My mom would use every square inch of paper when it would have been just as easy … easier actually … to go to a store and pick up some colored paper and pretty notepads.

None of the papers were exactly the same size and I thought that her outdated frugality was unnecessary and I silently scoffed at the ritual.

Years later, after mom was gone, Joe and I were visiting at my aunt and uncle's house - my mom's brother – we were discussing 'the old home place' where mom was born and I asked for a piece of paper to write myself a couple of notes. My aunt opened a drawer and brought out a pen with several small pieces of paper – each had been cut from formerly used paper and was stacked in the corner of the drawer. And there it was ... memories and shame flooded through me.

All these years later I was put in my place, realizing that my mom was not unusual but rather a part of a generation that had seen times I will never know. They were part of a culture of 'lack' and 'want' and yet a culture that had abundance, because they *knew* they didn't have to have 'everything'.

When I was a single mom with three little boys, my greatest fear was to not have enough money for heating fuel. It was the fear that my sons would be cold and then what would we do?

But I didn't understand that the *same fear* that impelled me to pay my heating bill in-full at the beginning of the Winter was the exact same fear that prompted my mom to cut up scraps of paper – the fear of lack. And why did it take me so long to realize that these are good lessons? At the time I couldn't step into her shoes. It took a long time before I realized that "Freedom is knowing what you can live without".

This morning my husband asked me to pick up a couple of things at the store for him – to remind myself I reached for a discarded envelope on top of the microwave...scribbled the list of items and tossed into my purse...several hours later retrieving the list...the memories returned.

Even though Mom's been gone for years now, her presence continues to teach me new lessons every day of my life.

If Mom were here in this present moment, I'd say to her "I'm sorry I scoffed ... now I've grown ... now I understand ... I'm sorry it took me so long. Please forgive me..."

"He Started It!"

"He started it..." I said, without realizing that others were listening.

It was a party that was in full swing since mid-afternoon with sunny backyard games and then a fresh fish fry. We have at least one fish fry each time John and Shannon come home to Minnesota. Shannon's parents, Rick and Kathy, are the best party hosts in the world! Shannon's brother and family were there, as well as John's two brothers and a mix of other friends and neighbors too. All of us were fed like royalty.

We were all stuffed and the party sprawled through the garage and driveway of their home. In the warm evening everyone had a drink in hand and the conversations were light and fun-loving. Some were in lawn chairs, while other people were floating from one group to another.

Seeing my husband, Joe, visiting in one group and my ex-husband, Mike, easily engaged in another group, the gal sitting next to me said with incredulity, "This is so amazing that *all of you* can be together and have such a good time! How do you do it?"

I suspected she had heard that we celebrate holidays all together. Perhaps she knew we all flew to Arizona for Christmas; my husband on one side of me and my ex-husband on the other ... maybe just all of us being there in one place at the same time prompted the question.

It was at this point that I openly said, "He started it".

And that's when things started to go quiet around us. At first just one of my sons was listening...and then another and then other guests stopped their conversation to listen as well.

So I continued. "After Mike and I were separated, he came by that next Christmas-time with several small gifts for me. At first I was angry thinking to myself 'I'm just going to throw these gifts in the garbage.' The gifts sat around for a while until a day when I thought 'Why not? Why not create a different kind of relationship?'"

"About six months later Mike was remodeling his house. He didn't put flooring in the boys' bedroom because he had already spent what he had budgeted for the project. The flooring was going to have to wait."

"I went to a carpeting warehouse and got a gift certificate, put it in an envelope, and at one of the boys next baseball games, I gave it to him."

"And thus began the creation of a whole NEW friendship; a whole new way of interacting ... a brand new way of looking at each other in a fresh light ... the light of mutual respect and support."

"He started it ... he offered ... and I accepted ... a peace treaty. What could have been antagonism became an alliance. Now looking back, I can't even imagine what life would have been like had we been feuding and fighting all this time...how much negative energy would it have taken on both our parts to hold onto old injuries?"

The gal who had asked the question still shook her head in amazement and said "I just can't imagine that!"

As the party went back to its small group conversations I said, "Well ... he started it ... and I am so glad he did."

2003

Rob had been gone from home for a while ... and then came back for a while.

Now he is leaving permanently.

How do I know?

Because his childhood blanket, the one he dragged with him constantly – the one that propped up his head to watch TV – the one that masqueraded as a pillow – the one that used to never leave his side - I found today; it was neatly folded and laid on the top of his empty dresser.

How do I know he isn't coming back? He didn't take the tube of toothpaste I bought for him. He didn't take the bottles of shampoo. *This time* he took just the things that he had *purchased for himself* ... he's gone.

Oh, I know it's time.

I am thrilled for his future adventures and I wonder what will become of me. How will my goals and dreams play out now that there is literally no one to divert my attention? I knew in my head that all three of my sons would grow up, but no one told my heart.

So today was the day – the day of cleaning Rob's empty room.

I put Robbie's old blanket inside a pillow case to wash it, so it wouldn't disintegrate entirely in the washer. As I write this ... the layers of ripped, paper-thin fabric is now laying gently over a lawn chair in the sun ... drying for what is the last time.

This blanket brings back 24 years of holding and cuddling and talking and laughing and tears and hurts and mistakes – all of it creating a bundle of twine binding the two of us together, that will never be separated.

As I walk into the sunshine and approach the, now dry, blanket – the tears fall as I fold the ragged pieces into something resembling a blanket. Finally, I can't help but put my face in its softness knowing that years down the road when I am gone, there will be a day when he opens a box in a closet to find his clean blanket and I know that then he will cry too – he will miss me.

Rob's *younger* brother called asking for his last three years of tax returns so that he can look at buying a house...my youngest son establishing a life.

Rob's *older* brother left his Knickerbocker bear on the desk in his room; the bear that stayed in the hospital with him when he was four and had an emergency appendectomy. Knickerbocker is sitting there looking very well loved. I am certain he wonders where his little master has gone. I didn't have the heart to tell him that he grew up. So I shipped Knickerbocker to Arizona so he could watch over my now grown-up son that loves him.

I did what I set out to do ... to raise three fabulous men and to watch and CHEER as they construct their own lives. Everything is happening exactly as planned ... perfectly ... then why is it sad?

I have the answer...

It's always sad when the fair is over ... when the rides shut down. It's so much fun while it's all happening; you just don't want it to end.

I wish I could love everyone in my life the way I love my sons.

I wish I could want happiness, success, and strength, for everyone else in my life as much as I do for them.

I wish I could care as whole heartedly about all humankind, as I do for these three men.

Maybe there's not enough room in a heart to love everyone like that.

Ageless Thinking

My aunt Eileen was one cool lady! She was the first woman I knew who wore pants. The first woman I knew who worked outside in the barn. The first woman I knew who could and would take charge.

She had standards and scruples. One time she was on a religious committee planning for a church dinner where food was donated by the members in her agricultural community. The priest knew how many pounds of butter was needed but decided to ask for more – saying that they could always sell the leftover butter. Eileen's sense of justice would not allow her to keep quiet. She challenged the man to do what was right and when he would not, she resigned from the group.

I had often heard Eileen talk of her wedding day – November 11, 1940 the Armistice Day Blizzard. I knew her memories were vivid, because her telling of the story was always the same, no embellishment, just the raw cold facts of the situation…being stranded in the car and her dad leaving them there with the promise to return with horses. In reality you couldn't see one step in front of you – and the man, my grandfather *did* return … somehow. There were 49 deaths on land and 59 sailors were lost on the Great Lakes, and yet Eileen lived to tell about it.

Through the years she talked about the things that hurt her … taking care of aging parents and being the one who was always there – the one that got overlooked. One day my grandparents were waiting for my dad to come to visit from 60 miles away and they heard the front door open to see Eileen…and I'm sure the words were not intended to hurt and yet the disappointed comment, 'Oh, it's only Eileen' came out unbidden and cutting. Every time I got a hand written letter in the mail from Eileen it was signed "It's only Eileen".

Living in an American Indian community, prejudice ran high in those days. Eileen and my dad were naturally very dark skinned and both tanned deeply when summer arrived. And yet Grandma and Grandpa had two other children with skin as white as snow. Eileen spoke of this to me specifically, I think, because of my dark skin inherited from my dad. And she told me that one time Grandma and Grandpa were invited to a wedding and they gave Aunt Eileen and my dad money and sent them downtown for the afternoon to buy candy. She said they took the two 'white beautiful 'children along to the wedding.

She was brutally honest about the priest coming to visit frequently as she aged. She would say "it's only because of the money". And we all knew she was right – there were others in this facility that were church members and the priest did not stop to visit with them. Likely her and her husband's money paid for a bunch of the church

197

remodeling project...the project that was ready for a grand opening at the time of my aunt's death...the project that would NOT allow my aunt to have her burial mass in the building ... because the church was perfect now and ready for the splendid 'grand opening' in just one week.

The final time I saw Eileen I knew would be my last. We talked in between other visitors. One lady brought fresh pears from her own tree and fed them piece by piece to Eileen. I had to have a taste too; I did not know such wonderful fruit would grow in Minnesota.

She had so much company in and out, I ventured to leave when she turned to me and blurted out "No, don't go!" Then she said "Oh I'm sorry!"

"No" I said "I can stay". And so I settled into the chair knowing that there was a comfort there that she needed...and so did I... a comfort of just being together for this moment.

On the night that was her last on Earth, I stayed up later than my husband. It was rare for me to be crawling into bed in the pitch darkness. Even though there are no shades over our windows, there was not a speck of starlight or moonlight. I didn't want to turn on a light so I followed the wall until I found the bed and climbed in quietly.

As I lay there shortly before midnight, a voice in my head said gently, "Open your eyes" and I thought to myself "What the heck! Open my eyes?" and the thought or voice or whatever it was, returned once again saying "OPEN your eyes".

When I opened my eyes, the bedroom was completely filled with light! I laid there for a long time just marveling at the soft glow in the room. I fell asleep at some point and awoke the next morning. Her son Terry called saying that precious Eileen had crossed over shortly before midnight.

I wish I could have been an adult, as a child, so I could have gathered more from her. She taught me more than I could ever foresee. I wish I would have recognized earlier, what a cool lady she was. There was no sense of obligation that took me to Eileen's door, that's for sure. I was always going home with more than I had arrived with ... and now I pick up the phone and wish that I could spend an hour in conversation with her.

While she was vibrant and healthy I took the opportunity one day to tell her what she meant to me. I let the words tumble out. I told her that I loved that she was ageless...her thinking was constantly evolving; she was always growing in awareness. I was saying all the things out loud to her that our friendship meant to me ... she just let me talk ... she heard all that I had to say, she let my words wash over her, I needed to say them and she wanted to hear them.

During her funeral service, in a town 15 miles away, in a church that *was not her own*, the priest said that Eileen would have understood why the mass wasn't held in her own church – and I smirked to myself ... if my Aunt Eileen were here in physical form, with a mouth to speak, she would have an earful to say to that priest right now!

I know that I will be with her again ... and we will laugh and talk as we used to do ... and if Eileen eventually meets up with that priest on the other side ... I *just want to sit back and watch...*

Without Words

The nurse in Memory Care forewarned us that my Uncle Delmar was not coherent most of the time. She said he sleeps almost continually and speaks not a word; that he gets his days and nights mixed up and comes out to eat at odd hours.

Joe and I were coming from his wife's funeral and I have no idea if my uncle was aware of this fact or not. It was afternoon, and even though I had heard everyone at the funeral saying Uncle Delmar was unaware, I could not leave town without seeing him one last time.

He was wearing daytime clothes and his bed was made for the day. Delmar was on the bed covered with a quilt pulled tightly up around his shoulders. I remember that he is like me, likes to feel tucked-in with heavy quilts and blankets. His wife had joked about this quirk, but I understood, because I am like him.

I pulled the quilt back a bit from his face and our eyes met. We stared at each other for a *long* time. Eventually I said "You know *exactly* who I am ... don't you?" And then he smiled. I put my hand in his and we stayed that way, just looking into each other's eyes. There was a communication there that was wordless, impossible to describe, even to myself.

Joe brought me a chair and then I laid my head on the chest of this man ... who spoke not a word ... and I did all the talking. I told him that my love for him is bigger than all the grains of sand in a desert ... taller than mountains ...wider than oceans. I talked about the 'Shit-eating' grin that was perpetually on his face and the natural curl that always hung down in the middle of his forehead. If I tried to sit up, he squeezed his hand tight around mine again, keeping me there. We smiled a lot at each other, eye to eye and heart to heart. Over half an hour went by; a silent wordless conversation.

He was still laying on the bed when we were about to step out of his room, he pushed the quilt back from around his shoulders, lifted his head and waved goodbye. He waved flexing the palm of his hand like a little kid, deliberately bobbing the fingers together up and down in unison.

As we stepped out of the room we saw the same nurse and she asked how Delmar was. I said brightly with tears, "Good! *Really* good!" She had a puzzled expression on her

201

face when she saw how happy I was, and yet sad at the same time.

I knew I was communicating with Delmar, and Uncle Delmar knew he was communicating with me, but I am quite sure no one else would agree … except for Joe.

Joe stood off in the corner of the room most of the time, just watching the two of us together. Joe saw us talking with our eyes … he watched us hearing with our hearts ... he saw the meeting of our souls ... having a private conversation ... saying our last farewell. I could see that Joe was moved by what he had experienced in that time of saying goodbye. And my husband knows ... I will love that man ... from now until the time ... he and I meet on the other side.

Ted From Iowa

I was taking a day off from work. Years ago, I rarely took a day for myself. I took a Friday off just for myself. It shouldn't sound monumental, but it was.

My husband works at the survey office for the county. Feeling excited to have a day all to myself, I stopped by my husband's office just to say HI and found it abandoned during coffee break time ...I waited for him to return.

In the office lobby walked a man who had several decades more living experience than I. Without hesitation he offered his hand and said, "Hi! I'm Ted from Iowa!"

I said "Hi Ted from Iowa, I'm Cathy"

Without exchanging last names, this high energy happy individual and I chatted as if we'd known each other forever. When Joe returned to his desk after coffee break I said, "Hi honey, this is Ted from Iowa, he's been waiting to talk to you about a land issue,"

Joe looked questioningly between this stranger and myself and asked, "How do you know him?"

I said, "I *don't* …we were just visiting while waiting for you." Since Joe obviously had work to do with this stranger, I left.

◆◆◆◆◆◆◆◆◆◆

Two days later Joe and I found ourselves escorting his parents to a family reunion. These were relatives, most of which Joe had never met. My normally outgoing personality was hesitating. This was going to be a whole group of people and I would know no one when we arrive. However, we had agreed to take Joe's parents and so we went. It was only 15 miles away after all … an afternoon picnic.

Helping Joe's mother out of the vehicle I looked around and surveyed the lake home location and the size of the crowd. Across the yard my eye caught a glimpse of someone familiar.

Without a moment's hesitation I called across the yard "Ted, from Iowa, what are you doing here?' He replied, "I live here, what you are doing here?"

This is crazy! How can it be? We are at a Zunker family reunion at Ted's house!?!

Within minutes we were introduced to Ted's wife, Joe's cousin Marilyn. You mean we are family?

And there it was... the beginning of a lifelong friendship.

I always say, "Strangers are just family we haven't met yet"... and this time … it was entirely true.

Interstate 35 at 65 MPH

I saw an amazing and, at the same time, hazardous scene this morning on I35 south of the Twin Cities. There were two lanes of traffic both directions traveling about 65 miles per hour and there ahead of me … traffic was at a complete STOP. I flashed my brake lights as I slowed, not wanting to get rear-ended.

I was three cars back from the stopped vehicle and looked to the roadside to see three adult geese and a brood of goslings looking frantic as they scuttled around the adults. Then I saw the dilemma. They were *walking* across the freeway. The adult mother goose was dead and bleeding on the highway. With traffic completely stopped the young woman who had killed the mother got out of her car. With bare hands and large sobs ... she lifted the broken bird and took her off the road.

♦♦♦♦♦♦♦♦♦♦

One of our trips to Arizona, I was riding with my son, John, when he unexpectedly pulled over to the side of the road, got out, stopped traffic and watched a turtle crossing the road; making sure it got to the other side; then he hopped back in the truck. To my surprise, our vehicle wasn't the only one that pulled over to make sure the turtle got across safely to shelter.

◆◆◆◆◆◆◆◆◆◆

I was enjoying the August heat as it flowed through my vehicle. Windows down, I was driving down a long country road lined with corn fields. At 55 miles an hour on the paved road, a squirrel carrying a small ear of corn still in the husk scurries onto the highway.

I'm saying out loud in the car "NO NO NO!" But the silly squirrel continues to run. I take my foot off the gas but my vehicle continues to glide down the road. I waited to hear the thud under my tires, but no, it never came.

Checking my rear view mirror I see the squirrel, knowing that my tires went on both sides of it. The cob of corn is in the middle of the road unharmed as well, and I see the squirrel pick it up once again – and I smile.

◆◆◆◆◆◆◆◆◆◆

"I saved a Yorkie today!" I said excitedly to my youngest son on the phone. My son has two adorable Yorkies of his own and I knew he would understand.

"I was driving down Highway 22 at 55 mph and I saw this little dog on the road. I came to a complete stop and waited ... until finally the little dog started running up a driveway.

There was someone working in the flower bed in the front yard, so I pulled in to tell the owner (grandmother puppy-sitter for the day) that the dog was on the road.

She said "All the way up there???" "Yes", I said as I crouched to pet the puppy, and the adorable ball of fur jumped right into my arms!"

◆◆◆◆◆◆◆◆◆◆

The animals are inviting us to slow down ... not just our *car* to slow down, but our continually speeding *minds*.

I am no exception.

The goose leading her family across the freeway is carrying on at the exact perfect speed for her goslings ... the turtle is on course to fulfill its destiny too ... the squirrel in the road was just getting lunch ... and the little Yorkie was out joyfully exploring the world.

So when I see an animal in the road I STOP ... I admire their steady paced life ... no matter what kind of life it may be ... and I ask for forgiveness ... for our outrageously hurried lives.

School Thanksgiving Lunch

It was Thanksgiving Lunch at Maggie's Middle school.

As my son John stood next to Maggie the vice-principal of the school came to meet him and said, "You must belong to Maggie". John smiled and said "Yes I do!"

The vice-principal told John what a lovely girl Maggie is. That she has a wonderful attitude and is friends with everyone. She also commented on the fact that as a new middle-schooler, each student got to choose an elective class. It could have been art or music and indeed one of the options was to work with the mentally handicapped. And this was the choice that Maggie had made; to be a peer tutor.

After getting their lunch, father and daughter went to find a table. When they entered the room, there was a table at the end of the area with only four people seated at it. There sat two mentally handicapped children …. one with a parent and the other with a grandparent there for the Thanksgiving festivities. The four were sitting by themselves. No one else was choosing to join them.

Maggie said to her dad excitedly "Dad! Let's go sit over there!" At the table Maggie proceeded to eat her lunch all the while chattering non-stop with the two other children.

There were tears in the eyes of the two other adults at the table as they watched Maggie interacting smoothly with the children that are always left behind ... visiting with the children that are normally not the chosen ones ... Maggie willingly accepting the ones that no one wants to have lunch with.

When they had finished their meal and were leaving the table, Maggie excitedly said to them "I'll see tomorrow OK? Bye!"

As John shared the experience with me, it didn't surprise me.

I thought back to a few years ago when Maggie and her mom and I, all three went on a field trip together for school. There was one little boy in the class who tended to wander, and that day the teacher that was chaperoning chose Maggie to watch over this little boy.

The classroom teacher clearly knew something about Maggie that I did not. I thought that I would have to help her with this responsibility. I was completely wrong. Every minute of that day Maggie kept track of her charge and watched over him.

Maggie's easy flowing actions at Thanksgiving lunch speak loudly to the world "Hey! Listen up everybody! *We are all people here,* people!"

I have no idea if her choices right now are leading her to a future profession. I have no idea if these experiences are defining moments in her life. What I do know is that Maggie is being true to herself right now! Maggie sees people as they **are** and allows them to simply be themselves. She definitely is *not* going with the crowd and choosing the 'popular' activities; if she were, the vice-principal would never have mentioned Maggie's uncommon elective choice.

Nobody has to teach her to be true to herself - she's not reading a self-help book to find her real nature - she's got it!!!! She is where all of us who care-too-much-about-what-other-people-think, wish we were ... right there ... being herself ...

C'mon Big Dog

After moving to Arizona it was Brady's and his parents first time back to Minnesota for a vacation. They were here at our home in the country and little Brady wanted to go to the apple tree to look around. Not realizing that there is more freedom for a child in the country, than in the city, his dad said "Well go!"

Brady looked amazed that he was free to roam. He looked at Hammer, our BIG dog, and laid his small hand on the strong wide back and said in a deep kid voice "C'mon big dog!"

◆◆◆◆◆◆◆◆◆◆

It was the first time Joe would be gone since I moved into our country home and I would be by myself. Hammer, our big dog, spent his nights in the front entry. I got into bed to read until I was ready to nod off. As I shut the light off I glanced out my bedroom door. There … stretched out full length blocking the entire doorway to the bedroom was our massive dog. He lifted his head slightly and looked at me as if to say "I think I'll stay right here tonight." I didn't argue.

♦ ♦ ♦ ♦ ♦ ♦ ♦ ♦ ♦ ♦

One night when I was alone I called Hammer to come into the house. He was getting old and slow but wouldn't come inside. I couldn't find him. This break from routine made me uneasy until I discovered his location. Peeking out the window I watched the rabbits playing in the muted light of the yard. I could see Hammer inside his kennel, patiently watching in the shadows, up against the wall of the house … pacing back and forth … waiting uncomplainingly. Now that his body is slowing down – his mind has to work smarter to replace the speed he once had.

At 6:30 the next morning I heard some banging and bumping going on. It sounded like the quick movement of say a...rabbit? But the only way to get in the garage was through the doggie door! Oh come on! Nothing is stupid enough to go IN the garage through a doggie door!

This slow nearly crippled 105 pound animal with hip problems had captured and killed a rabbit. But I knew it was coming ... he was biding his time ... I knew that someday he would make a surprise move and end up with a rabbit. Hammer looked up at me with guilt on his face and I said "You can have it. Anything that dumb deserves to get eaten."

♦ ♦ ♦ ♦ ♦ ♦ ♦ ♦ ♦ ♦

Hammer sleeps on the other side of a common wall that separates our bedroom from the garage. Now the garage is equipped with *handicapped ramps* to the doggie door going outside ... and a *handicapped ramp* to the landing that enters the house ... there's a dog mattress ... there's a

212

gigantic doggie pillow ... all of it nearly blocking the door. Add a 105 pound dog on top of it all and the door is impenetrable. His hips are worn out. He can only hear high pitched whistles now ... so he lives in a comfortable, quiet, peaceful world.

At 4:30 one morning, I awoke to sounds of sporadic thuds in the garage *once again.* Knowing full well that the dog makes no sudden moves anymore, I knew something else must have entered through the massive doggie door. I never thought to put up a sign saying 'dogs only' in order to keep other dumb critters from entering. So, I lay in bed listening and wondering. When morning arrived I heard Joe astonished to find a baby rabbit dead at Hammers' feet.

It had to be suicide, I thought, the only way Hammer was going to capture a baby rabbit was for it to voluntarily lay down its life.

I hear Joe saying soft and gentle powerful words of wisdom to the dog, *"If you kill all your friends, you won't have anyone to play with!"*

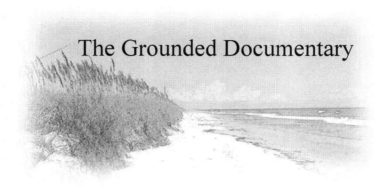

The Grounded Documentary

2013 and Joe is harvesting all HUGE potatoes this year, over 600 pounds and only one bucket of small golf ball size.

I stand at the kitchen sink scrubbing the outside of a spud that is **four** times the size of my hand getting the last of the dirt off it …coming from the earth less than 48 hours ago trying to scrub off every speck of soil.

It reminds me that I loved making mud pies when I was a girl. Mom's discarded pie tins or anything else that we could find became a mold; mixing dirt and water, packing it into a shape, decorating with leaves or flowers and then letting it dry in the sun. I always feel right playing in the dirt.

◆◆◆◆◆◆◆◆◆◆

I took my preteen sons to a friend's house. The 'old' man who came walking from the garden wearing country clothes had a freshly pulled carrot in his grasp. He quickly swiped his hand down the length of the carrot and proceeded to take a big healthy crunching bite, dirt and all.

My sons being polite said not a word…until we got in the van and were driving out the driveway. "Did you see that!?!" they asked with total amazement in their voices. "He took it out of the ground and it still had dirt on it! And he ATE IT!"

I was proud of them for just watching and waiting to discuss it in the safety of the vehicle…processing what they had seen. I know they thought the man was on the verge of craziness.

◆◆◆◆◆◆◆◆◆

Maggie age 5: One time when Maggie was in MN I took her with me to dig carrots in the garden...she was EXCITED. My city raised grandchild thought they were going to come out of the ground looking as they do in the grocery store. When she saw them she said "Euuuwww! They're dirty!"

Maggie age 7: One day my granddaughter wanted the two of us to go have our fingernails done...I told her to set those thoughts aside ... we were going to plants flowers and play in the dirt.

◆◆◆◆◆◆◆◆◆

Me grown up: A girlfriend called one sunny early Friday afternoon. I had just gotten home and was heading for my garden to play. She wanted to know I if I wanted to go shopping. Let me see, let me think about that for just a nanosecond, given a choice between garden and shopping ... no contest. Shopping is going to lose *every* time!

215

◆◆◆◆◆◆◆◆◆◆

Fast forward decades…I am listening to an audio book by Andrew Weil called Spontaneous Happiness –a powerful book about changes in our society … what are the things we have lost or set aside because of our ever improving society…and Mr. Weil speaks to the fact that few of us are outdoors any more – that many of the antibodies that used to protect us from colds and infections are *in the soil* – that there is now *dirt therapy for children* – a time for them to play in the dirt because there are things missing from bodies now, that were once protections. Perhaps a bit of *dirt in our body is* not such a bad thing after all.

I smile, remembering the day my sons saw the old man eating a carrot directly from the ground.

◆◆◆◆◆◆◆◆◆◆

Fast Forward to 2016:　　(YouTube The Grounded Documentary Full Version)

The ground has always been … well … grounding for me. Something in my being draws me to it. It's nothing I've been able to explain; it's more of a feeling of health and well-being. Maybe it's just as simple as body movement and sunshine. That is what I always thought anyway, until a girlfriend shared a link for The Grounded Documentary … now … there it is … proof.

If you choose to watch it … get ready to forever change
ew of dirt.

Crying Together

I have an old 'dog-eared' photo from years ago. My twin sister had come to Minnesota from Iowa with her two sons. It was a rare occasion to have the five boy cousins together for several days of play time.

The day came for my sister and her sons, Tim and Jim, to go back home. The sadness filled us all and soon the boys, *all five of them* began to cry. This was not just a little cry, but huge big bear sobs. I took a picture of those sobs. The touching sight in the photo still brings tears to my eyes. Once one child had started, they were all easily led to the table of tears.

Why do children cry when another gets hurt? I saw it in my daycare all the time. One baby cries and just the sound of it brings another baby to tears. One child skins their knee and cries, and within seconds waterworks are puddling in the eyes of another child. Then another child will begin to cry as well, for no reason! At least, there is nothing physically wrong with them to make them cry, nothing that is, except for the fact that someone dear to them is hurt or wounded.

Children have soft hearts and they can easily empathize with others even though the majority of their world is self-centered.

It had seemed to me to be a thing confined to kids, until I saw the same occurrence at the funeral of my nephew. Yes, he was one of the five children in the old 'dog-eared' photo.

At the funeral, each time I watched my twin sister cry, I too would cry. Why? Because she had lost her baby ... because she was hurting terribly ... because there was nothing I could do about it ... except to cry with her. I will cry with her forever over this loss.

We, as adults are exactly the same as children, except that we have bigger bodies now and bigger hurts. We still cry when those we love get hurt...still hold their hand and hope to heavens it will somehow help. As adults, our sufferings have a more helpless sensation to them. We know that there is no Snoopy Band Aid to cover the sore and masquerade it as a cartoon character...it is an open wound. Just like children crying together over an injury or a disappointment, we too cry together ... those tears create a bond between us in a deeper way than we knew possible. The tears cried together create a chemical reaction ... one that becomes sticky like glue ... it becomes a bonding agent that forever joins those two hearts together.

Our Greatest Fear

Our greatest fear is not what we *think* our children are going to do – our greatest fear comes from knowing what stupid, idiotic and dangerous things WE did as a young person!

There are things my sons keep from me and I'm glad they do. These are the times, when years later we look back, with horror on our faces saying, "I could have been killed doing that! I was so lucky!"

Every adult I know has said those words or words that mean the same thing.

We know that our children do these things...have to do these things as we did and we silently say a prayer that they too will be the lucky ones...that they will live to see the day of their own wide-eyed wonder, looking back on the risks they took.

And what about now? Have those long-ago risks made us chickens?

Have those perils from our youth taken away our motivation to try something new or to accomplish those things we know deep inside we have the talent to achieve? Or do we get lazy and use the excuse that it's not worth the risk? Telling ourselves, we are just being cautious.

Is it possible that **not** using our talents is taking a risk too?

"Our deepest fear is not that we are inadequate. Our deepest fear is that we are powerful beyond measure. It is our light, not our darkness that most frightens us. We ask ourselves, who am I to be brilliant, gorgeous, talented, and fabulous? Actually, who are you *not* to be? Your playing small does not serve the world. There is nothing enlightened about shrinking ..." Marianne Williamson

I have read this quote many times and each time it makes me shudder. I quake because I know I am hearing *truth*. The risks of our youth are about doing things that are dangerous or hazardous. The risks in adulthood are completely the opposite; the risk of doing *nothing* with *the brilliance and talent* that are inherent inside.

And so I pause each time I bump into this quote ... taking a moment to evaluate ... mostly waiting a minute to *feel* if that shudder arrives ... if it *does*, I know I am not taking advantage of what I have been given ... if I do *not* shudder and I feel a sense of contentment inside ... then I smile.

Unbidden

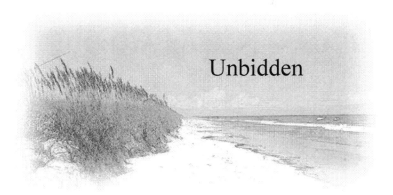

They'd been married for 61 years and he got married *late* by his generation's standard. He was 25 years old when he married the woman of his dreams. That means he's 86 years old!! Wow, they just drove from Seattle to Minnesota for a family reunion and they make the trip every year.

Normally there is no one else in the car to witness the yelling and bickering. She is hard of hearing, along with early stages of "forgetfulness". He drives, she navigates. To get their point across to each other now it has to be done *loudly*. This particular year – 2008 – a daughter and grandson decided to hitch a ride with them across the country to attend yesterdays family reunion.

Everyone was sitting in chairs, at outdoor tables, on a perfectly mild summer day in the Midwest. I ended up sitting at the table with this man and his daughter. His wife was at a different table and involved in another conversation.

He reminded me so much of my dad that I gravitated toward him like an industrial magnet holding me there next to him. I asked him about his working years. He said, "It's been nineteen years since I retired and I am so fortunate to have this." Twice as we talked, I irresistibly, reached over and touched his deeply tanned forearm, which reminded me of my dad.

I wanted to monopolize his time but soon, he was wandering from table to table to greet others at the reunion. Only his daughter was now across the table. We chatted for several minutes until I finally spoke the unbidden truth that tumbled out of my mouth.

"I see people with mansions and beautiful things, but really in my life, I almost never desire what they possess. But I will tell you the truth. Sitting here today ... watching you sit at this table with your dad ... I am jealous to my core. To the very center of my very soul I am totally and completely jealous". With misty eyes I said, "What I wouldn't give to have my dad back for an afternoon, sitting beside me at a table, in a chair, in the Minnesota sun."

She looked taken aback, even stunned, but there was nothing I could do to keep the words in! Then she moved to the chair right next to me, as she saw the "missing dad" filling my eyes.

She sat quietly for so long, I wished I hadn't spoken.

Then almost in a whisper she said, "You know, I needed to be reminded of that. Mom and Dad have been bickering on the whole trip and at times I just want to tell them to 'grow up'! I needed to remember how fortunate I am just to have them. Thank you."

Sometimes, words come falling out of my mouth ... at times I try to hold them in and I cannot. I don't know what to call it when that happens ... sometimes I think that it is not *me* that needs to say them, as much as it is someone else needing to *hear* them ... and without my permission, *their need to hear these words*, is actually pulling them out of my mouth into reality.

Or maybe it was a simple reminder for me that I loved my dad ... and maybe that simple reminder just needed to be passed on to her ... while she still has her dad ... sitting right there beside her.

The Best Man's Shirt

Have you ever screamed out loud in a UPS store? I have ... and this is how it happened.

◆◆◆◆◆◆◆◆◆◆

I was in the office this morning and I had time before my next appointment, so I decided to get out and stop by some garage sales and enjoy the sunny day.

Just last night, we had taken Robbie to Fargo for a flight the following morning to Panama City Beach Florida where he would once again be the Best Man in a wedding. This was Rob's 27th wedding as either a groomsman or a best man.

At the garage sale Robbie's ring tone came from my phone. I was surprised since I was sure he was busy lying on a sun drenched beach!

I asked casually "Hi! What's going on?"

He said "Well, I'm hoping that maybe you can help me. I forgot my shirt for the wedding.'

There was this sinking feeling in my gut. I knew the clothes had been purchased for the wedding over a year ago - there was no way for him to go and buy one at a local shopping center.

He wanted to know if I could go to his apartment, get the shirt and overnight it to him. I had about 40 minutes before my next client was going to be in the office. The guy running the garage sale knew something had just happened as my face changed and I almost *ran* to my vehicle, realizing that the wedding was starting in less than 24 hours.

Rob's apartment was two blocks away. I had a key. He said the shirt was aqua blue.

In his apartment I grabbed a bright blue and white swirled shirt with short sleeves - beach attire I thought - from his closet. I took a picture and texted it to him as I was pulling into the UPS parking lot.

Robbie called again and said "That's the ***wrong*** shirt!"

I hustled back to his apartment and finally found the appropriate long sleeved shirt in a beautiful blue aquamarine color. I told him the name on the tag as I was rushing back to UPS.

"Yes!" he said "That's it!"

There was a young lady behind the counter and an older lady at a computer working. I burst into the UPS office with the shirt on a hanger and I said "This needs to be in Panama City Beach Florida by tomorrow morning at 11:00 AM... can you do that?"

The younger gal behind the counter said "yes".

She gave me an address label to fill out and immediately took the shirt from me, folded it, and put it in a mailer ... sealing the envelope.

UPS could get it there by 11:00 tomorrow morning for $111.86 or by 1:30 tomorrow afternoon for $84.00. Robbie said 1:30 was cutting it too close; the wedding was at 2:00.

On the phone, once again, Rob asked me to send a picture of the second shirt and I told him the package was already sealed and on its way. I was sure it was the right shirt - the name on the tag was the same as the other groomsmen ... but there was that ounce of doubt floating in the air.

When the transaction was finished, I stood in the middle of the UPS Store, looked at both ladies and asked "Is it alright if I scream?" Both women laughed and agreed it was fine.

Like a kid beginning a tantrum and laughing at the same time I barked "For crying out loud! What was he thinking? He's the Best Man!" And both of the ladies laughed and so did I.

I had three minutes before my next appointment was supposed to start ... I could just imagine my client standing in the hall at my locked office door.

Nope ... I got back to my office to find that my client was late. About 20 minutes later she arrived apologizing profusely ... and I did *not* tell her the story.

Finishing at the office I decided to finally get to the garage sale and I sent Rob a text message saying, "OK I'm done at the office now and I'm going to go to the garage sale that I was supposed to go to earlier and I figure if I find anything there that I want to buy, *you might be the one* offering to pay for it since I saved your butt! LOL I love you babe! "

The response that I got back to the text message all by itself was worth $111.86   "I'll buy you anything you want. Since this is the one-millionth time you've saved my butt. I can't thank you enough. I'm so lucky to have you. I wouldn't be half the man I've become without you. I love you!!!!"

I went home happy at the end of the day ... and I told NO ONE.

The next day Joe and I were traveling for the weekend and I waited with my cell phone in hand ...and waited ... and waited to hear from Rob. Finally the text message came through. "It's here! And it's the right shirt!"

I still told no one.

After Rob had returned home Joe and I and Rob went to lunch together. He was wearing a casual aquamarine blue short sleeved shirt - exactly the same color as the wedding shirt. Now I understood ... he had packed the wrong shirt.

What was crazy was how the dominos fell into place ... I was free when he called ... the garage sale was two blocks from his apartment ... I had a key ... the UPS store was three blocks away ... and my client was late.

It's so fun when you get to be the one coming to the rescue and it all falls into place. But I know I wouldn't have wanted to be in Rob's shoes ... on the 'waiting' end of the delivery. I'm sure it put a haze over his good time, wondering and waiting for the next day's package. But he had taken charge and got it figured out ... and that's the way he is with everything else in life too. That's why he's ... the Best Man.

Brian & Kelley's Wedding

In two weeks this young man will be a groom and then a husband for the rest of his life ... and he will be a good one in both cases. I know this already for I have seen his heart – his dedication to the human race in general. Without a moment of hesitation he asked me "And WHY aren't you and Joe coming to the wedding?"

Brian is one of my 'other' sons; one of those young men that I would gladly claim as my own.

Later that evening Joe asked me "Why AREN"T we going to that wedding?" I replied, "Because you said you wanted to get some Fall clean up done that weekend". We glanced at each other as we both realized that yard work could wait and we made travel plans to the wedding of a young man we could easily call a son.

We explored Black River Falls Wisconsin (the home town of the bride) a bit before the wedding. Oktoberfest was in full swing as it rained lightly... Joe willingly ordered a stout oatmeal beer as we watched local townspeople in their annual celebration. Just by seconds I missed photographing a musician playing two horns at the same time – and playing them well!!! We could have easily melded into the town that night as everyone was in the frame of mind to drink more beer and to make new friends. Almost reluctantly we rushed to the hotel to get ready for the wedding.

And there they were ... a groom and three groomsmen looking more elegantly tailored than I had ever seen! Obviously the bride (whom we had not met yet) had wonderful taste, not just in clothes but in men as well.

My son Rob, the best man, was signing the documents after the ceremony as I rushed to the front to take photos. Without turning his head I heard Rob say, "Is that my mom?"

Well of course it was his mom! Who else would it be? The photographer stepped aside politely so I could have my turn at taking a photo!

Later, at the reception, my son, the best man, gave a toast and began by saying, "My best friend is here tonight – that's my mom sitting right over there."

I was dumbfounded as I heard the words coming through the microphone. He continued, "She told me one time...that sometimes souls have known each other for a very long time – like she and I have known each other before. And when Brian introduced me to Kelley for the very first time, I couldn't quite put my finger on what I was aware of – then I realized, I knew the first time I met her that *she was the one*, that she and Brian have known each other a *very very* long time and are meant to be together forever. So if you will all raise your glasses, this is a toast to Kelley and Brian ... together forever."

As my son returned to his place at the head table, I began to breath – I hadn't realized I was holding my breath. I had just received one of the biggest honors of my life ... there was no fanfare – there was no applause – there was no confetti falling from the sky, but there it was ... my prize. The gift of a feeling ... the gift of words spoken ... the gift of love.

A Head on His Shoulder

Joe and I spent New Year's in Arizona at John and Shannon's home, so I already knew that Maggie's (my granddaughter) fish in the fishbowl was not looking good. It was hiding a lot under the bridge in the bowl and after we arrived back home to Minnesota, I received a call from Maggie saying her fish had died.

I felt bad for her, and at the same time she was calling, she and her dad were about to go and buy another fish. I asked her about the fish that died. She said, "We're not going to flush it down the toilet. It's raining here in Arizona and we can't bury the fish until the rain stops. So we put the fish in a plastic bag and put it inside a plastic container in the freezer to bury it another day."

It was an emotional low for her, having the fish die, and she doesn't know yet, that just around the corner is going to be something wonderful happening that will offset the previous low ... it's a temporary pre-teen roller coaster ride ... and it's all going to level out soon.

232

****

One day recently John went to Maggie's middle school and asked the staff to have Maggie brought to the office.

Maggie came to the office and was curious because school wasn't over for the day.

She said to her dad, "What are you doing here?"

With a smirk on his face John replied "What!?! ... Can't I come to school to pick up my daughter?"

As the two of them went to his vehicle, an hour before any of the other students would be released. Maggie's sense of anticipation began to grow... She asked, "What are we going to do?"

John said, "It's a nice day, how would you like to go and feed the ducks?" And that little girl part of her was delighted! So the two of them went to the grocery store to buy bread and each a box of candy to snack on.

The two of them fed all of the bread to the ducks, sat down on a bench to eat their candy, and in a quiet moment Maggie leaned her head over and laid it on his shoulder.

And somehow I know that the feel of that, not-quite-yet-teenage head on his shoulder ... will never go away ... that he will hang onto it forever ... for safe-keeping ...

Maggie will remember ... there was a dad who took time off from work ... a dad who took his daughter out of school ... a dad who creates balance on that roller coaster.

Chicken Pox

John was 19 and in college, two hours away, at the time his young son, Brady, had Chicken Pox. While Brady was sick, John was driving back and forth to Fargo each day so each night he could sit with his sick child in his arms. Brady would lay miserably motionless the two of them sharing the gloom. All during that time of misery, there was an equally pained, miserable expression on John's face, as he provided as much comfort as possible.

I watched an unbreakable bond being formed in those days. Before the Chicken Pox Brady loved and enjoyed his father. After the Chicken Pox there was *trust* at a different level … it was a guarantee ... an endless pledge that had been formed.

◆◆◆◆◆◆◆◆◆◆

One time a little boy in my daycare had Thrush – a terribly uncomfortable condition in his mouth. The poor little guy was miserable. It lasted so long that it was impossible for the parents to take time off from work, and so I held him day after day in every free moment at daycare.

We would sit and rock together as other children played around us. Only when necessary, I would set him down in order to attend to other children's needs or cook lunch. He never cried when I set him down, somehow he knew that I would be back immediately when my tasks were attended to. His misery lasted several weeks. Slowly and surely the bond between him and me meshed as he healed and soon he didn't want to go home with his mom. He had found comfort in my arms.

As the years went by in daycare, invariably a parent would ask if I could take care of a sick child that was not contagious. I certainly agreed and yet I would tell them up front … the most significant bonding time in the life of a child is when they are hurting – and who do you want them to bond with?

Now as I look around I find the same thing is true with big people. Big people want all the same things ... to be held ... for us to share the same pained miserable expression on our face as they are wearing that day; to give them reassurance that this will get better.

I recognized the bond between people doesn't come from amusement parks and high priced vacations. Oh sure, they're fun ... *anybody* can do that ...but *anybody* can play together - *anybody* can go on vacation together - that's easy.

You know who you can trust when the 'other things' in life are going on ... when there's work to be done ... when a crisis arises ... when you are sick ... or feeling broken ... like when you have chicken pox ... and your dad holds your sick and miserable body in his arms. That's when you know for sure ... who is always there for you.

Bank Account

Perhaps I would be well advised to listen to the things I tell every client in my hypnotherapy office. I tell everyone that the subconscious mind nearly always drops a negative. So if you are telling yourself "<u>don't</u> eat sugar; <u>don't</u> eat sugar; <u>don't</u> eat sugar" the subconscious drops the "don't", so in reality what you are actually telling yourself is "eat sugar; eat sugar; eat sugar".

This lesson was blatantly obvious to me one day when Joe and I were at our son Tom's house. His driveway was elevated on one side with a drop-off. Railroad ties formed a retaining wall that was flush with the concrete ...so if you got close to the edge, with the passenger side of the vehicle, one could potentially just slip a tire or two off the edge of the driveway.

I volunteered to move Tom's car, all the while repeating in my mind "<u>Don't</u> drive off the edge - <u>don't</u> drive off the edge - <u>don't</u> drive off the edge."

I focused closely on the drop off side of the driveway ... and of course what we focus on becomes our reality. In a matter of seconds I was in trouble ... I knew that two tires were partially over the edge and if I did something stupid, like panic, I could end up with some big damage.

So, I stopped ... just stopped completely ... checked my mirrors, assessed the situation and through my open window called for assistance. Tom and Joe calmly looked at the situation. I got out of the car. With one of them driving and one giving a few directional hand signals, it was a matter of 30 seconds and the entire situation was corrected without incident.

Tom had a girlfriend at the time. When she saw what had *almost* happened she said to me wide-eyed, "If I had done that, Tom would be really *mad*!"

I took her words to heart and even though I had apologized at the time, I called Tom once again a couple days later and again said that I was sorry.

What he said to me was insightful.

He said "Mom, if there are bank accounts in life, with all you've done for me, you've got a BIG balance to draw on. It would take a lot more than this to even begin to use up that balance. There was no harm done ... so now, forget about it."

He is right, it is all about bank balances ... saving ... making withdrawals from time to time when you make a mistake ... when we do something stupid.

Hopefully the older I get, the fewer withdrawals I will make, as I *put to use* the lessons I have learned along the way. And sometimes when I'm not sure what to do in life ... when I'm not sure how to solve an issue ... I try to remember to just STOP ... even if the tires are slightly over the edge ... just STOP before any real damage is done.

STOP and ask a trusted friend to see what I can't see at the moment. STOP and say I'm sorry where it is needed ... And then ask that trusted friend ... to give me just a few hand signals ... helping me to get back on the road.

Maggie April 2016

Six days at John and Shannon's house in Arizona with ONE task; spending time with Maggie.

My granddaughter's parents are going on vacation, leaving the two of us together! Mags still has bunk beds in her room so she and I will be able to share a room, one more time – talking to each other as we go to sleep.

One other time, years ago, when we were bunking together, Maggie caught me in the middle of the night on my iPad as she crawled out of bed to go the bathroom. In the morning she whispered to me in a conspiratorial tone, "Grandma, I saw you last night on your iPad!" I whispered back, "Don't tell anybody OK?" She agreed.

So, for this trip, I am making a list now of the things we will do together while this country grandmother is in the city. I said definitely **not** to Maggie's suggestion to have fingernails and toenails professionally painted. We will be doing painting of our own.

I had a set of wooden serving trays shipped to her house. In my suitcase will be lettering and decals for the trays

Varnish will be involved. A set of wooden blocks we'll be painting and then making into a castle. I will be taking sunflower seedlings through security at the airport in a plastic coffee container, so we can plant together and watch something grow. We will be baking and learning a bit of chemistry as we do.

There is magic in spending uninterrupted time together. I will be watching her play volleyball and taking a hundred pictures.

And, (drum roll here!) unbeknownst to her, there will be horseback riding for the very first time. Months ago on the phone Maggie asked if I would take her horseback riding. I sidestepped the question saying I had no idea how to make that happen.

Later, I was making plans to see a good friend while in AZ, and my friend asked if I would like to bring Maggie to the ranch where she boards her horse, to see the baby horses. I casually asked if there was any chance Maggie could *ride* a horse. She said yes, that her husband, Juan, would happily lead Maggie through the riding areas on a horse for the very first time. My list of plans and activities were all falling into place perfectly.

Shortly before my trip, Maggie said to me on the phone, "I won't need to go to afterschool care when you're here grandma, because I *know* **you're** going to want spend every minute with **me!**"

Ding ding ding ding ding!!!!! **That** was the bell of truth I wanted her to know for sure ... **that** is the thought I always want in her mind ... I want to spend every minute with her ... no matter what that minute might look like ... if that minute includes happy stuff, wonderful! ... if that minute includes sad stuff ... I'm there.

That's **all I've ever** wanted her to know ... that I'm there ... for every minute.

Rock Star

This was my dream vacation and Joe made it all come true. Standing hours outside in the cold, you'd have thought we were waiting to see a *rock star*!

Well, he is a rock star of sorts ... in my mind anyway. By the looks of the line of well-dressed people standing outside in 32 degree temperatures, I'm not the only one that thinks so. Outside for 3 hours on a cold Georgia morning, watching the sun rise, I was wearing dress clothes and high heels waiting to be 'scanned' by Secret Service agents before seeing Nobel Peace Prize Winner and former President of the United States, Jimmy Carter.

Arriving at 7 AM at Maranatha Baptist Church in Plains, GA, we thought we would be early for the opening of the doors at 10:00AM, until we found out that, new friends we had made two nights earlier, had arrived at 4:30 AM.

In actuality we were *so late* that the director of the affair said we may very well end up sitting in an overflow room watching the President on a monitor. I chose to ignore her comment and thought to myself, 'There is no way I came all the way to Georgia to sit in an overflow room.' So we waited in line.

It was President's Day weekend that happened to fit into our personal travel schedule and it never occurred to us that there would be larger crowds because of the holiday, having additional events on Monday, President's Day.

As we stood in line a Marine with a German Shephard directed the dog to every vehicle in the parking lot, sniffing all the way around each car. Everyone was asked to leave personal belongings in the trunk of their vehicle to ease the burden of getting through Secret Service on the way into the building.

Before we arrived in Plains we spent hours in the Atlanta Presidential Library. Behind glass was the Nobel Peace Prize he had been awarded in 2002. A bulletin board gave visitors the opportunity to leave a note for the ex-President and his wife. There were 3 x 5 recipe card size papers on the table in front of the board. When the bulletin board was full, people would take the push pin out of a note, put theirs on top, and push the whole stack back onto the board. Some of the pushpins held 10 to 15 notes. Overflowing with comments, all of them said the same thing or words to the same affect: thank you, for what the two of you have done for the world.

We had toured his boyhood home. Room by room, there was a button in each room that played a voice recording of Jimmy Carter sharing memories. In the bathroom of the house his recorded voice described the exposed water pipe going up the wall, then across the ceiling, with a bucket with holes hanging on it for a shower head.

There were vegetables growing in the garden and chickens in a pen at his boyhood home. A park ranger said that often times he will look around to see Secret Service entering the property and then Rosalynn and Jimmy Carter coming to get vegetables or fresh eggs together. He said that everyone who works on the property is respectful, letting them have a scrap of privacy, as they live a small town normal life as much as possible.

Joe had booked hotel rooms in Americus, GA at an old mansion turned into hotel just 15 miles from Plains. Looking up three stories to balconies from the lobby, it was a Southern buffet for the imagination. On one of the outdoor balconies we met a couple from South Carolina. He had grown up in Georgia and his school bus driver, when he was small, was Jimmy Carter's mother, Miss Lillian.

The train station in Plains was Carter's campaign headquarters and had been chosen because it was the only public building at the time that had a bathroom.

So we wandered the Georgia countryside and met people. We ate peanut butter ice cream and boiled peanuts. We bought raw peanuts to bring home.

After all that we had seen and experienced we were now, finally, waiting outside the church; assistants counted the people in line, trying to figure out who would fit in the sanctuary where the President would speak and who would go to the overflow room.

As we stepped in the front doors of the church we were scanned by Secret Service and then told that we would be sitting in the choir area *right behind the podium*, ten feet from where the President would speak.

With no fanfare at all Jimmy Carter entered and asked the military in attendance where they were from and then the non-military. There were people from all over the world ... to hear the man whose global influence grew after he left the White House. He talked about the Carter Center and its accomplishments and goals and then smoothly flowed into Bible teachings. When he was done he was escorted out of the room for a 10 minute break.

After break he returned with Rosalynn by his side for the worship service. The two were seated in the third row, now facing us, as the service commenced.

The process of picture-taking afterwards was swift and efficient. Jimmy and Rosalynn were seated and smiling as couples or groups posed behind or next to them for a quick photograph. After our photograph, we visited briefly with a Secret Service agent on the front step of the church,. He said that he has been with the Carters for two years now... that you never know in his line of work, when a change in assignment may come. Then I asked him, "Will you write a book about your experiences, as others have done in the past?" He said "No Ma'am, these memories are mine to keep."

Joe and I went downtown for more peanut butter ice cream. Sitting in our rental car in front of the grocery store, devouring the treat, we saw a three vehicle caravan coming fast toward main street from the direction of the church ... two black SUVs with smoked windows and a white lead car coming to the intersection ... *not* stopping at the stop sign, and turning in the direction of the Carter home. Clearly, the picture taking was over.

10 days after arriving home, I received a package in the mail from the couple who got to the church at 4:30 AM.

They had been able to stay for Rosalyn and Jimmy Carters' Presidents Day presentation at the high school where the two once attended together. Afterwards the President stayed on stage to sign books, while his wife went to another room to do the same. He would sign as many as three books per person. Inside my package that day was an autographed copy of A Full Life by Jimmy Carter.

Reading the book was like a walk through our vacation all over again ... when Jimmy Carter wrote about butchering hogs, we had seen where the hogs were processed - when he wrote about the commissary on the property - we had been there too.

The day that Joe said we were buying airline tickets to Georgia, I was thrilled and looking forward to hearing Jimmy Carter speak. I had no idea that I would be coming home with so much more than I could have ever imagined.

We had walked and talked and discovered parts of the Presidents life he willingly shares ... we had made friends ... and explored the Georgia countryside ... no one talked about politics ... it was all about humanity. The church was filled to overflowing with people showing respect to a man and a woman who have offered their 'after White House ' years to serve the world.

The Carters are still building Habitat for Humanity houses. When asked why, Jimmy Carter replied, "I can't think of anything better to do."

These two humanitarians make no apologies for the faith that guides them ... they make no apologies for the White

House influence that has enabled them to do more than most ... over 90 elections in 37 countries have been benefited by the Carter Center ... The Carters spend their time promoting global health ... they spend their energy encouraging conflict resolution in situations around the world.

Their intentions are clear ... the betterment of *all* humanity ... and the one concise principle all these accomplishments stand on ... the glue that holds it all together is ... love one another ... now, that's ... a rock star.

For the Love of Gloria

I don't even know how to write this story; certainly it's the longest I've ever written. Even though I lived one of the characters in this story, it's still hard to write it, to try to put the pieces in some semblance of a puzzle that actually creates a picture when you're done.

This is the frame of the puzzle: My beautiful Aunt Gloria married and divorced the same man twice. In between these marriages she twice gave birth, (in two different states, one year apart) to a baby boy and gave both for adoption. Fifty-some years later, the older one looks on the internet for his biological mother. At the same time the second son's aunt is searching the internet for the second son's biological mother.

First son does not find mother, but rather finds younger brother.

Then, first son finds his biological mother's brother (his biological mother, Gloria, had passed years ago) and asks

249

for verification that the signature on the adoption papers is authentic. They are. First son of Gloria tells uncle about second son of Gloria.

And so this story is written from three different geographical locations, ending with welcoming two whole new families into our lives...it was easier than you might think....

One year ago...near Springfield, Illinois

Searching internet records for his biological mother, the thought that Dave might have a younger brother...a man who looked just like himself, had never even entered his mind...

Dave, a chief of police outside of Springfield, Illinois goes about his business taking care of the needs of the public, while his wife, Nancy, teaches young children at a nearby school ... the two of them together, have raised two sons and now enjoy a grandson. It is a life filled with meaning and connection, filled with challenge and purpose and accomplishment. The police chief and the teacher were high school sweethearts. They went to prom together...she being every ounce a princess and he, a prince charming. (I saw the pictures, it's true!)

The fact Dave had been adopted by his parents so many years ago was of little interest or concern to him until one fateful day. Nancy, sorting papers and documents from a box that came from Dave's parents' estate, held in her hand ... Dave's adoption paper with the distinguished signature of a woman named Gloria...

His curiosity took him to the internet to search for a biological mother whom he knew nothing about...not even her medical history. Perhaps a medical history alone was reason enough to begin ...why not just search a while on Ancestry.com? Why not just write a couple of letters? You never know what you might find...

Early 1960s near Odessa, Texas

Being told they could not have children was undoubtedly distressing news, to the young Texas couple. After many late night discussions they decided to approach their minister about privately adopting a baby through the arms of the church. They reminded the minister of his promise to help them adopt a child, shortly before the minister transferred to a new assignment in Albuquerque NM.

Three days after arriving in Albuquerque, NM, the minister sat working at his desk with his office door open. That fateful day, a gracious young woman entered, saying she was pregnant and could not keep the child. The woman's name was Gloria...

The church gave Gloria lodging and the young couple in Texas paid for her expenses and medical bills throughout the pregnancy. Without her family's knowledge or support, Gloria gave birth to a baby boy on Christmas Eve.

Knowing the couple in Texas would make loving responsible parents; Gloria's Christmas Eve baby was given over to the loving arms of adoptive parents in Odessa Texas on the 26th of December. These, now happy parents, went about their life centered on their son.

The hand of the Divine was generous ... after adopting their son; this couple gave *birth* to two children...both blond and healthy. The adopted oldest son, Tim, brown-haired and brown-eyed, would often say to his mother, "I want an *older* brother!" But an older brother was not to be ... not yet, anyway.

Gloria, through my eyes...

The 1960s was the beginning of speaking openly about difficult subjects. A time of questioning long held beliefs and expectations. But it came slowly to my family as it did to the nation as a whole. There were often topics deemed to be embarrassing or socially unacceptable and they were spoken about only in hushed secretive tones.

I remember hearing my mom quietly mention my Aunt Gloria (her younger sister) had divorced her husband. That was unheard of. How could this be? Of course my mom wasn't talking to me. I was too young to be involved in such a private conversation, but not too young to overhear things that were none of my business.

Gloria's husband was an incredibly handsome man, that's all I knew about him, for I doubt I ever spoke a word to him face to face ... his photo was all I knew. They lived a long way away...in Montana for a while I think ... and Alaska too. It might as well have been another continent as far as my sheltered country perspective was concerned.

Aunt Gloria had grace and poise. I admired her for being a working woman when most women I knew stayed at home all day. Gloria's clothes were glamorous too! The fact she had asthma only added to her mystery. She carried an inhaler with her everywhere! Like a movie star that had a long cigarette holder, to me it seemed like a sign of high society, my aunt Gloria and her inhaler! The years between her trips back home to Minnesota only made that mystique grow.

The whispering continued as the years passed by and I heard in hushed tones that my, now single, Aunt Gloria gave birth to a son and gave him up for adoption. I overheard someone say she lived with her sister's family in Illinois until the birth of the child. That's all I knew ... that a child was born...

Years later, I heard the news Aunt Gloria was remarrying her husband. There! Now everything was all right in my fairy tale world. Now, they will live happily ever after!

The colors of that pop-up fairy tale book faded into a second divorce.

And the final whispers were the worst of all – the story of breast cancer ... I saw her once after that diagnosis, looking healthy and strong ... and then at the age of 48 she was gone.

She had married the same man twice, but what had happened in between those marriages? No one will ever know. In my mind's eye, I see a love story like Titanic. A story of adoration and passion with a tragic ending...or maybe it wasn't so tragic. Maybe it was a love so deep, she refused to share it with others. Maybe it was so precious; she carried it in her heart for safe keeping, not allowing others to tarnish an affection she held so dear.

My sister, Pat, always kept saying we had to find Gloria's son. She said we had pictures of his mother that belonged to him as a keepsake. Pat spent money to find this son of Gloria's, not knowing that private adoptions were more difficult to follow. I didn't think there was a chance we would ever find him. I felt a nagging going on inside of me every time Pat mentioned the search. I wanted reassurance that Gloria's son had been raised in a loving home, and cared for deeply, as she had intended.

December 2012...

In stunned silence I sat staring at my computer screen. My fingertips curved above the keys, but my fingers would not move ... could not move.

Emails had been jamming my Inbox ever since Uncle Craig received a letter in the mail from a stranger in Illinois.
The stranger gave Uncle Craig his email address.
The stranger said he had been searching for his biological mother, Gloria. The stranger had been born on the day in 1960 that Gloria had given birth to a son.

Now comes the final shock; the stranger said that while searching for *his* biological mother, he found *another man* searching for the same mother.

My mind reeled! There are two? Aunt Gloria gave birth to two sons?

Now the second stranger, in Texas, joined the email conversation. He said his Aunt Betty, who is a genealogy guru, had been searching for his biological mother. Searching for the Gloria whose signature was at the bottom of his adoption papers. While Aunt Betty searched she found the first stranger in Illinois looking for the same Gloria. The second stranger in Texas sent a copy of his adoption paper to us, Gloria's family.

I opened the document. At a glance I knew ... there was absolutely no doubt. I stared at Aunt Gloria's elegant scrawl at the bottom of the page. One adoption form from Illinois, and now the second one (Christmas Eve 1961) from New Mexico…15 months apart. No father listed on either.

Now this second stranger waited for Uncle Craig to respond to the question. "Is this your sister's signature?" It wasn't my place to answer. I sat staring at the computer screen waiting … and waiting … and waiting … Uncle Craig needs to answer … the heart-wrenching question being asked, "Was your sister, my mother?"

My uncle's resounding email popped into the inbox. "Yes it is!!!!!" he replied to Gloria's second son.

I sat at this computer, the one I am using at this very moment, with fingers poised above the keys, trying to let it all make sense …Gloria had two sons, they found each other, and now they found us! Come on!!! Where is Oprah when you need her?

I needed to respond to this email quickly. Somehow, I knew from the tentative tone of the second stranger's email -- the second adoption, that someone, somewhere, waited … holding their breath. Someone at the other end of this email address had to be wondering … is this too much for a family to believe? Will they just turn away? Will they say, 'Let sleeping dogs lie' 'Leave well enough alone' or 'Turn a blind eye'?

I sent an email to Dave (Illinois), my new cousin and to Tim (Texas), my new cousin … welcoming them with shouts of joy to our family and telling them what their biological mother had meant to me.

Throughout the next week, Dave and Nancy (Illinois) and Tim and BJ (Texas) started sending photos of themselves and their families to all of us … some when they were growing up and some current... I watched and looked for signs of Gloria's features. The baby pictures of the two men were astonishingly similar ... like twins at times. Finally B.J. asked for pictures of us...dah! We had sent pictures of Gloria and it hadn't occurred to me they didn't know what the rest of Gloria's family looked like. Soon, cyberspace was filled with family photos and memories of Gloria...

A few weeks later, on Christmas Day, I called Dave and then Tim. I didn't want to interrupt their Christmas festivities, but I wanted to hear their voices, I wanted more than an email connection ... and wanted to tell them Gloria's whole family is waiting to welcome them.

For Dave and Tim ... the reality of these discoveries had to be slowly sinking in. Two brothers living over a thousand miles apart and not knowing the other existed. The older brother that Tim had always asked for ... had become a reality. When would they meet each other? When people asked, "What did you get for Christmas?" did Dave and Tim say, "Oh nothin' much really ... just a *new brother*!"

And we discussed a more somber thought that leaves one thinking about fate, destiny and the hand of the Divine. Had Gloria chosen to raise her sons, both would have been orphans in their mid-teens.

As for me, I told _everyone _about the upcoming reunion in July, then, still months away! "I have two new cousins!" I would announce. "We knew there was one, but we got TWO! Isn't that amazing?!" Leaving the hair salon one day, the stylist called after me, "Thanks for the story! I really needed that today!"

Several months later Dave and Tim met each other face to face. They brought their families on vacation and met in Branson. The rest of us got to see all of the pictures from their meeting and couldn't wait for our turn! At the end of July, a weekend gathering of family was planned at Uncle Craig's and Aunt Joyce's house in St. Paul for all of us to finally meet our new cousins.

Meeting our cousins (St. Paul, MN July 2013)

On a Tuesday night in mid-July, Joe and I dressed for a summer theater performance. In the car, I put my hand to my throat and said to Joe, "Well, this is the last time I will ever wear this necklace." He looked quizzically at the pearl necklace as I fingered it. "Why?" he asked. "Because" I said with tears in my eyes, "this was Gloria's necklace, and next weekend it will go to her sons. I have simply been holding it for these past decades until her sons were found."

I had never told Joe this was Gloria's necklace. I never really told him much about Gloria at all. I never thought the day would come when I would actually meet Gloria's son, and now to find there are two ...

That night after the theater I went to my jewelry box to find a keepsake of my grandmothers,(Gloria's mothers') from the early 1900s, a choker made of black onyx stones and rhinestones with matching clip-on earrings ... I remember Grandma wearing it. When I would wear it people would think it was new, because it's back in style now ... the new, made to look old. But this is the real deal, it isn't made to *look* old, it really *is* old. Now there were two keepsakes for two cousins. One from Gloria, and one from Gloria's mother. Gently I packed the heirlooms, knowing it would be a meager offering ... because we couldn't give them what

257

they really searched for…we couldn't give them Gloria. We couldn't give them answers to their questions …

FINALLY, the Friday arrived to go to St. Paul. I said to my husband as I spread my arms out wide, looking at the clear blue sky. "Joe ... look all across the whole wide world today ... look at every single person on the earth … and know that *no one in the whole wide world is going to have a better weekend this weekend than we are!*" I was going to meet two new cousins.

He smiled at me…he knew I had cried many times awaiting today … Gloria's sons …wow!

This weekend was going change all of us – from Texas to Minnesota to Illinois and people from states in-between.

We booked a room at the same hotel our cousins were staying at. After arriving, I paced…are they too tired to meet us? Has it been too emotional of a day already meeting my Uncle Craig – THEIR uncle Craig for the first time? And so I paced…and Joe and I went for a walk on the bridge…until finally I could stand it no longer…I called their room. They said they would be right down to the lobby.

My heart pounded watching the elevator doors open as four people- two couples stepped off. We all started to reach out to shake hands and then didn't even bother … we are family … we hugged and searched for a quiet comfortable area away from the Friday night sounds of the hotel lounge.

I sat there thinking, 'I will never forget this night … meeting four people who were instantly family'. After hearing about their lives my biggest question was answered; had the hand of Divinity guided them both to

258

loving homes as Gloria had intended? The answer was, YES. I slept peacefully that night knowing Gloria's sons had become brothers, and now we are officially cousins.

The next day was the large gathering at Uncle Craig's and Aunt Joyce's house in St. Paul. I wasn't the only one searching for treasures that had belonged to Gloria to give to her sons. My uncle Craig brought out the oil paintings of Jesus in the Garden that their mother, Gloria, had painted. There were tears in everyone's eyes as our patriarch gave the paintings to Dave and Tim. We offered these two men a small part of their mother, a woman we all loved and adored.

One cousin brought an elaborately decorated cake with a picture of the two cousins on the cake welcoming them. There were decorated cookies with the names of our new cousins. There were photos albums other cousins brought filled with pictures of Gloria through the years.

We passed around photo albums Dave and Tim brought from baby to adult ...monumental moments captured. It was easy to see these two men were twins, simply born fifteen months apart.

Saying good bye Sunday morning was heart wrenching...we had just come together and now we were saying good bye. So this is an ending and beginning at the same time...the end of a search and only the beginning of a relationship that has changed us all...none of us left the same as we came.

The Monday after our weekend together I had to pretend I was the same person I was on Friday of last week – but I was not. Just months earlier we had never even heard of Dave and Tim and now we are family. I saw a powerful side of people… acceptance and love and hope … and that hopefulness for humanity runs through my veins even greater than ever before ... knowing ... all people are my cousins… really.

I hope Gloria saw it all ...

…saw the loving families who raised
her sons from birth …

… saw her sons welcomed into our families loving arms …

… and saw her sons … become brothers.

The Dance Card

Although the bride is not my daughter, it feels that way. She and her siblings grew up side by side with my sons.

Since John and Shannon are in Minnesota and are attending the wedding I made it mandatory that my other two sons come as well. I have the right ... I'm the momma.

It's rare for me to have more than one drink, but today, at the wedding reception, I asked my husband to be prepared to drive us home. I was enjoying my wine with dinner and I planned to have more as the dancing continued.

My boys take good care of their momma in every respect. After the wedding dinner, the dance began and my third-born beautiful perfect child, danced with me early in the evening, a slow song. He said in my ear, "Momma, I miss you – we don't get to spend that much time together these days".

He had grown up and always makes me feel special.

Later in the night I decided to have just one more glass of wine and approached the bar laying my $10 bill on the counter and asked the bartender for a glass of Merlot.

When the bartender returned with wine in hand he said, "The man at the end of the bar is buying this for you".

I looked down the length of the bar as my eyes rested on my oldest son; my first-born beautiful perfect child. I raised my glass, smiled my gratitude and walked away overwhelmed at what the bartender had said. I wanted to scream "The man at the end of the bar?? The man at the end of the bar!?! That's my son! ... He had no right to become a man without my permission!"

He had grown up and always makes me feel special.

The last dance of the night was a slow song, of course. It has to be a slow song, if it were wild and rowdy, the crowd would call for more until the DJ would have to relent. So, my second-born beautiful perfect child is waiting for the opportunity to fill my dance card. His huge arms surround me as we float and he sings the words to ♫ The Keeper of the Stars ♫ in my ear. "It was no accident - Me finding you - Someone had a hand in it - Long before we ever knew"

He had grown up and always makes me feel special.

If I chose these men before I arrived on Earth ... I didn't just do *well*, I rocked it!

If indeed "it was no accident" that I get to spend this lifetime with them ... then I planned well ... and maybe they planned well too ... choosing each other as comrades ... like choosing your side on a little league baseball team ... wanting your best friends beside you ... to grow up with ...

I don't know about that ...I do know ...
                                I hit the "mother-load!"

262

About the Author

For you to know who I am...
...ask me who I love
...ask me who my heroes are
...ask me what lessons have touched
the very core of my being.

I am fascinated with how people think,
why they do *what* they do,
and why the world is the way it is.

My education is from a university ...
my wisdom is from *life*.

In my perpetual quest for *truth,*
I am like Socrates the great questioner.

With every step I take
I am like Plato the lifelong learner.

I write to connect hearts,
hoping to find *myself* in the process.

Small monumental moments happen every day...
right in front of me ... with every step I take.
I don't want to miss even one instant, for it is the
connecting of these seemingly insignificant fragments,
that a meaningful existence is created.

This I know for sure.

Cathy Weber-Zunker

Cathy is a hypnotherapist in Alexandria, MN with specialty certification in Brainwork's Recursive Therapy, General Anxiety Disorder and Smoking Cessation. www.cathywz.com.

Copies of Cathy's first book Travels on the Yellow Brick Road; Lessons Learned on the Path to Oz are available on Amazon.com.

35411034R00148

Made in the USA
San Bernardino, CA
23 June 2016